Success guides

Standard Grade
Administration

Kathryn Pearce ✕ Carol Ann Taylor

Contents

Preparing for assessment

Introduction to business organisations

The working environment

Storage and retrieval of information

Reprographics

Sources of information

Preparation and presentation of information

Travel

Exam technique

Exam-style questions and answers

Index

Assessment

The Standard Grade Administration exam assesses two elements – **Knowledge and Understanding** (KU) and **Problem Solving** (PS) at Foundation, General and Credit levels. All pupils sit the General level plus one other level – either Credit or Foundation. You will be awarded the higher grade achieved from the two levels you sit. The length of each exam is:

- Foundation level – 1 hour
- General level – 1 hour 15 minutes
- Credit level – 1 hour 30 minutes

A third element of the course is the **Practical Abilities** (PA) project, designed to assess your ICT skills. This is a series of integrated tasks (undertaken at either F, G or C level) which is marked externally. About 15-20 hours of class time is allocated for this.

The overall award for the course is calculated on the average grade for each element. KU accounts for 30% of your final grade, PS accounts for 30% and PA accounts for 40%.

Revision

Know the course requirements

- Make sure you know exactly what to revise – ask your teacher for details.
- Make sure that you have course notes for each unit.
- Divide the course into units and sections; then work through these 'manageable chunks' one at a time.

Organise yourself

- Produce an exam revision timetable, allowing revision time for other subjects as well. Spread your subjects over the week and only spend short periods of time on one subject at a time. Allow regular breaks while studying.
- Attend supported study classes offered in school – this allows you access to the full range of resources available in the classroom, including your teacher!
- Pace yourself during the exam period – you need to rest between exams. Don't cram – 'little and often' is a much better approach to revision.

Revision methods

- **Note cards** – work through your 'chunks' of revision and make notes on small note cards to make it easier to learn key points.
- **Mind mapping** – create a mind map diagram where you identify all the key points and can visually see the links between key points.
- Work through **past papers** – one of the best ways to prepare for any exam is to look at what has been asked before, in what way and how often. You may see that the same types of questions appear regularly.
- Work with a **friend** – go over key points on note cards or mind maps, or work through past paper questions together.
- Do questions **against the clock** – so you know you can do them within the appropriate time.

Practical Abilities project

You will do the Practical Abilities project at Foundation, General or Credit level. Attempt a project at the most appropriate level for you – you only have 15-20 hours to do the project, making it very difficult to change level at a later date.

Your teacher cannot help you complete any of the tasks, but you can use any previous notes given, tasks undertaken and help guides available. These are valuable resources that you **should** use to gain the highest possible grade.

The PA project takes the format of a task book in which a scenario is set, for example, you may be an Administration Assistant for a record company. You should work through each of the tasks in order. Ensure you read the question very carefully before starting and note **all** the instructions (printed in boxes). For example, a word processing task may contain the following instruction:

> Use a variety of fonts, bold and italics to enhance the document. An appropriate graphic should also be used.

In this case ensure you have used at least two different fonts, bold and italics at appropriate points. Also make sure you have included an **appropriate** graphic, such as a musical note or a CD (for the record company scenario).

General hints when completing the PA project

- Include a **formulae copy** of your spreadsheet if required – many marks are lost because candidates forget to include them.
- Label all graphs appropriately (include an explanatory key if relevant).
- When recalling/making changes to a database do not overwrite your original copy.
- In recall tasks, your recall task must relate to the original with the only changes being those specified in the recall task.
- Ensure that all text can be read – widen columns if necessary.
- When keying in e-mails and other tasks which require your own wording ensure you use accurate and business-like wording (text talk is not acceptable).
- Where tasks require particular information to be highlighted, for example, internet printouts, it is important that you do this, otherwise you will be awarded no marks.
- **Always proof read** all your work – candidates lose marks unnecessarily because they have not checked through their work carefully. Use the spell check function, but remember this doesn't pick up all mistakes. You still need to carefully check all of your work to ensure there are no keyboarding errors and that you have followed all instructions.

Top Tip
Ensure **all** tasks are submitted in order, with your name, school and task number on each printout. A declaration with your signature must also be completed.

Top Tip
The importance of accurate keyboarding and checking your work thoroughly cannot be underestimated. **Always check all of your work!**

Organisation of departments

What is an organisation chart?

An **organisation chart** is a diagram, usually displayed in the **reception** area of an organisation, which shows:

- the names of the **main departments**
- the **job titles** of employees
- the **management structure**
- the **reporting structure**
- the **relationship of staff** within the various departments
- the **span of authority** of managers.

The reporting structure

The layout of the organisation chart allows employees to see who they are **responsible** to and **accountable** for, and whom they have **authority** over. It also shows the employee who they **report** to if their immediate line manager is not available.

Benefits of organisation charts

Benefits to customers and visitors

- Gives a better idea of who to contact within the firm
- Gives an idea of the type of work carried out by the organisation
- Gives an immediate impression of the overall size of the organisation

Benefits to employees

- The reporting structure is clearly shown
- Shows the **chain of command**
- Shows the **span of control**
- Overall size and structure of the organisation is easily seen
- Promotion channels can be identified
- Helps new employees learn about the firm and the type of work it does.

Top Tip

In an exam if asked who would be contacted when an immediate line manager is not available, just use your finger to follow the line upwards to find the person on the next level of the organisation chart.

Top Tip

Exam questions often ask the benefits of an organisation chart to either **employees** or **customers/ visitors**. Always read the question carefully and tailor your answer to the requirements of that particular question.

Terms associated with organisation charts

Chain of command: the passing down of instructions from one level to another.

Span of control: the number of employees each person/manager is directly responsible for.

Wide span of control
- **Many** staff report to one manager
- Delegation of manager's tasks would be necessary

Narrow span of control
- **Few** staff report to one manager
- Easier to supervise staff and monitor work of all staff under manager's control

Level of responsibility: the position of the employee within the organisation. For example, the Sales Manager is positioned above sales department staff because he/she in charge of them (and has authority over them).

A **line relationship** is where members of staff report to the person immediately above his/her level. An employee is accountable to his/her line manager, that is, they must undertake the tasks delegated to him/her. The line manager is responsible for the employee(s) directly below him/her on the organisation chart.

A **lateral relationship** is where members of staff have the same level of authority – they are on the same level of the organisation chart, and cannot delegate tasks or give instructions to each other.

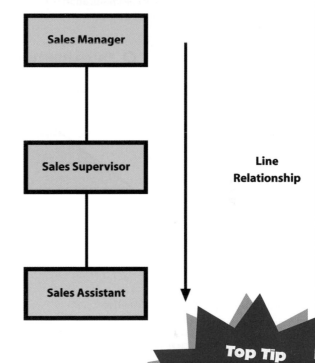

Line Relationship

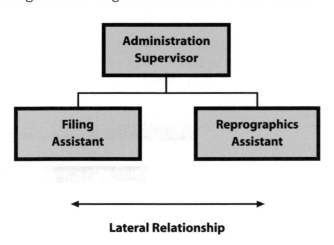

Lateral Relationship

Top Tip
Learn definitions of key terms associated with organisation charts as they are often asked as exam questions.

Quick Test

1. What information is usually shown on an organisation chart?

2. What are the benefits of displaying an organisation chart (to both customers/visitors and employees)?

3. Explain the term 'line relationship'. Can you think of any members of staff in your school who have a line relationship?

4. Explain the term 'lateral relationship'. Can you think of any members of staff in your school who have a lateral relationship?

Answers 1. Names of main departments; job titles; management structure; reporting structure; relationship of staff within various departments; span of authority of managers **2.** Shows customers/visitors: contact names; work done by organisation; size of organisation. Shows employees: reporting structure; chain of command; span of control; size of organisation; promotion channels; helps new employees learn about firm. **3.** Where members of staff report to the person immediately above their own line, e.g. Headteacher and Depute Headteacher. **4.** Where members of staff have the same level of authority in the organisation, and cannot delegate tasks or give instructions to each other; e.g. two teachers of Business Education

Tall and flat management structures

Tall and flat management structures

○ **Tall management structure**
- Many levels of management posts
- Many lines of communication
- Narrow span of control

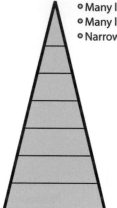

○ **Flat management structure**
- Few levels of management posts
- Wide span of control

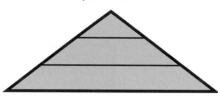

Top Tip
Learn 2 advantages and 2 disadvantages of each type of structure.

Tall management structure

Advantages
- It may be easier for managers to supervise staff
- There are more opportunities for promotion
- May lead to more motivated employees who understand their very specific roles and responsibilities

Disadvantages
- Employees may not feel involved in decisions made at top management levels
- Employees may not get the opportunity to show initiative
- Many highly paid management positions mean that it may be costly to run the business

Flat management structure

Advantages
- Employees may be more motivated as they are able to show initiative
- Decision making is less complicated and probably quicker
- Team-working may be developed and strengthened

Disadvantages
- Increased workload of employees may lower staff morale
- Fewer opportunities for promotion
- Wider span of control may become unmanageable

Quick Test

1. Describe the differences between a flat management structure and a tall management structure.

2. What are the advantages and disadvantages of a flat management structure?

Answers 1. Flat: fewer levels of management posts and a wider span of control; tall: many levels of management posts and a narrow span of control **2. Advantages:** employees may be more motivated as they are able to show initiative; decision making is less complicated; team-working may be developed and strengthened; **disadvantages:** increased workload of employees may lower staff morale; fewer opportunities for promotion; wider span of control may become unmanageable

CREDIT

Organisational restructuring

Reasons for restructuring

- **Growth:** An increase in the amount and/or range of goods the organisation produces may mean additional staff are required.
- **Downsizing:** To reduce costs the number of staff employed may be reduced without a subsequent reduction in the number of goods produced.
- **Delayering:** To reduce management costs certain layers of management posts are removed. This would lead to a flatter management structure.
- **Outsourcing (Contracting out):** To reduce costs of employing their own specialist staff yet benefit from specialist advice, an organisation may buy in the service of another company or individuals to undertake specific duties in the short term.

Possible benefits and problems of restructuring

Benefits
- Reduced costs due to downsizing (particularly staffing costs)
- Improved efficiency – fewer channels of communication, faster decision making
- Outsourced specialised tasks may be done more quickly and to a higher standard
- New roles enable staff to show initiative – improved motivation

Problems
- Low staff morale (as employees fear for their jobs)
- Resistance to change – staff may be unhappy with changes and therefore be unmotivated
- Initial communication problems and uncertainty over roles may arise
- Costs of restructuring

Use of organisation chart after restructuring

A new organisation chart would be useful for showing the **changes** in:
- the size of organisation
- the chain of command
- the span of control of managers
- relationships between employees (line and lateral relationships).

Quick Test

1. Why would an organisation consider restructuring?
2. What are the possible benefits and problems associated with restructuring?
3. Why would an organisation chart be of particular use after restructuring?

Answers 1. Growth, downsizing, delayering, outsourcing. **2.** Possible benefits: reduced costs if downsizing; improved efficiency; outsourced tasks done more quickly and to better standard; improved staff motivation: possible problems: low staff morale; resistance to change; initial communication problems; costs of restructuring. **3.** Chart would show changes in: size of organisation; chain of command; span of control; relationships between employees

Functional organisation of businesses 1

Organisations are arranged so that related activities are carried out in the one area. These key areas of activity are called **functional areas** (or departments). Functional areas commonly found in organisations are:

- Human Resources/Personnel
- Sales (and Marketing)
- Finance
- Purchases
- Computer Services (ICT)
- Administration.

Each functional area is organised with the employees at the top having more responsibility than those at the bottom.

Human Resources/Personnel Department

This department is responsible for dealing with the people within the organisation – recruitment, training and development, staff welfare, and conditions of service.

When recruiting staff, the department follows this process:

- **job descriptions** (providing the applicant with information about the job – job title, salary, working conditions, etc.) and **person specifications** (providing the applicant with information about what qualifications, experience, skills, etc. are required) are prepared
- **job vacancies** are advertised
- **application forms**, job descriptions, and person specifications are sent out
- completed application forms are received
- short lists of applicants are completed, interviews are held, selection is made
- letters are sent to successful and unsuccessful applicants
- applicants may be asked to enclose a written statement from a **referee** about their suitability for the job
- the successful applicant will be issued with a **Contract of Employment** (giving details of the job title, salary, working conditions, etc.) once they have started work.

Induction training is provided for new employees to introduce them to the structure and people in the organisation and to advise them of health and safety regulations, workplace practices, etc. A training programme may also be in operation for all employees to upgrade their expertise or to retrain in a different area of work. Training may be carried out within the workplace – **on-the-job training** – or employees may attend external training courses, for example, at college – **off-the-job training**.

The Human Resources/Personnel Department must ensure that:

- employee records are kept up-to-date – this may be done manually or using a database
- a record of all accidents is maintained
- a healthy and safe working environment is provided
- employees are kept up to date with health and safety/employment legislation.

Job title	Main tasks/activities
Human Resources/ Personnel Manager 	• reports to the Board of Directors on issues relating to the HR/Personnel Department • is responsible for overseeing/monitoring/motivating employees within the HR/Personnel Department • interviews applicants/carries out staff appraisal • issues warnings/dismissals/promotes employees
Administrative Assistant	• word-processes letters to successful and unsuccessful applicants • files application forms • updates and maintains employee records

Other job titles within this department include Recruitment Manager/Assistant, Training Manager/Officer/Assistant, Trainer, Employee Relations Manager, and Health and Safety Manager/Officer/Assistant.

ICT may be used within this department to:

- maintain employee records – database
- key-in letters to applicants/memos to employees – word processing
- record employees' absences/holidays – spreadsheet
- transfer applicants' details on to computer – scanner

Quick Test

1. What is a functional area?
2. What document provides a job applicant with details about experience required?
3. How can applicants' application forms be transferred onto computer?

Answers 1. An area where related activities are carried out – a department. 2. Person specification. 3. By scanning them

Functional organisation of businesses 2

Sales (and Marketing) Department

This department is responsible for dealing with the sale of goods produced by the organisation. It will carry out market research for (new) products and also advertise products made by the organisation.

The Sales Department follows this process when selling goods:

- it receives **letters of enquiry** (asking for the price/quality/delivery times)
- it issues **quotations** (providing details of price/quality/delivery times/discounts)
- it receives **order forms** (requesting to purchase goods)
- it issues an **advice note**
- it requests the Finance Department to prepare and issue an **invoice**

If at any time goods are returned then a **Credit Note** (details what goods/quantity/value were returned) is issued.

Job title	Main tasks/activities
Sales Manager	• reports to the Board of Directors on issues relating to the Sales Department • is responsible for overseeing/monitoring/motivating the employees within the Sales Department • sets sales targets/analyses sales figures
Sales Supervisor	• deals with customer enquiries/complaints • monitors/assesses the work of the Sales Assistants • reports to the Sales Manager on a regular basis
Sales Representative	• visits customers and potential customers to encourage them to buy the goods
Marketing Manager	• identifies potential new customers and products
Market Research Assistant	• gathers information on potential new products, for example, by questionnaire • analyses data from questionnaires
Administrative Assistant	• word processes quotations/price lists • files order forms • updates customer records

Other job titles within this department include Sales Assistant and Advertising Assistant.

Top Tip
When describing a task carried out by an Administrative Assistant in a specific department you must make reference to that department. For example, it is not enough to say the Administrative Assistant in the Sales Department updates records – you must make reference to customer records.

ICT may be used within this department to:

- store customer records – database
- key in quotations/price lists – word processing
- prepare advertising leaflets/posters – word processing
- record sales figures – spreadsheet.

Finance Department

This department is responsible for all the money coming into and going out of the organisation. This includes employees' salaries and wages, paying suppliers, receiving payments from customers, and petty cash.

The Finance Department must consult and check with other departments to ensure that financial information is correct, for example, Purchases Department (to pay suppliers), Sales Department (to request payment from customers), and Human Resources/Personnel Department (to calculate employees' wages).

The Finance Department uses the following financial documents:

- **Invoice** – a document which provides information about goods which have been bought on credit and informs the buyer how much is due
- **Credit note** – a document which provides information about the cost and reason for goods which have been returned
- **Statement** – a document which provides information on a regular basis about spending, returns, payments and how much is owing
- **Cheque** – a document which is used to make payment for goods.

Job title	Main tasks/activities
Finance Manager	• reports to the Board of Directors on issues relating to the Finance Department • is responsible for overseeing/monitoring/motivating the employees within the Finance Department • prepares budgets and forecasts • controls spending of departments • prepares final accounts
Administrative Assistant	• word processes letters to customers for non-payment • prepares cheques to be sent to suppliers • takes cash/cheques to the bank • checks/files invoices • updates financial information on the spreadsheet

Top Tip
An advantage of using a spreadsheet is that calculations can be carried out automatically and accurately using formulae.

Other job titles within this department include (Financial/Management) Accountant, Finance Clerk, Wages Assistant, and Invoice Supervisor.

ICT may be used within this department to:

- calculate employees' wages – spreadsheet
- prepare budgets – spreadsheet
- prepare letters to customers for non-payment – word processor.

Functional organisation of businesses 3

Purchases Department

Top Tip
Always refer back to the question when completing your answer. This ensures you don't forget what the question is actually asking.

This department is responsible for dealing with all purchases into an organisation, whether raw materials, stationery or office equipment.

The Purchases Department follows this process when buying goods:

- it sends **letters of enquiry**
- it receives **quotations**
- the 'best buy' (dependent on price, delivery, time, discount, etc) is selected
- **order forms** are completed and sent to chosen supplier
- a **goods received note** (to check that correct goods and quantity have been received) is received with the goods
- an **invoice** (checked against goods received note, calculations checked and passed to Finance Department for payment) is received
- finally, a statement is received.

If at any time goods are returned then a **credit note** (details what goods/quantity/value were returned) is received.

Job title	Main tasks/activities
Purchases Manager	• reports to the Board of Directors on issues relating to the Purchases Department • is responsible for overseeing/monitoring/motivating employees within the Purchases Department
Buyer	• negotiates contracts • agrees purchase price and conditions
Administrative Assistant	• word processes letters of enquiry • completes and sends order forms • files information from suppliers – catalogues, price lists

Other job titles within this department include Stock Controller and Warehouse Supervisor.

ICT may be used within this department to:

- store supplier records – database
- key in letters of enquiry – word processing
- record issuing and receipt of stock – spreadsheet.

Computer Services (ICT or IT) Department

This department is responsible for dealing with all ICT issues within the organisation. Employees within this department are responsible for installing new software, making sure that licences are up to date, maintaining computer equipment, training employees how to use hardware/software, responding to ICT problems, creating and issuing user identifications (IDs) and passwords, and managing the network.

Job title	Main tasks/activities
Computer Services (ICT) Manager	• reports to the Board of Directors on issues relating to the Computer Services (ICT) Department • is responsible for overseeing/monitoring/motivating the employees within the Computer Services (ICT) Department • maintains the network
Computer/ICT Technicians	• is responsible for setting up computers • maintains computer equipment • deals with hardware/software problems

Other job titles within this department include Analyst, Programmer, Computer Operator, and Help Desk Operator.

Administration Department

This department is responsible for providing a range of office services and administrative support to all other departments within the organisation, including:

- word processing – internal and external documents
- maintaining databases and spreadsheets
- filing
- mail handling – manual and electronic (e-mail/fax)
- reception duties
- reprographics facilities
- purchase of small stationery items.

Job title	Main tasks/activities
Administration Manager	• reports to the Board of Directors on issues relating to the Administration Department • is responsible for overseeing/monitoring/motivating employees within the Administration Department
Administrative Assistant	• word processes (letters, memos) • makes travel arrangements • organises manual and electronic diaries

Other job titles within this department include Filing Clerk, Mailroom Assistant, Receptionist, and Reprographics Assistant.

Centralised administrative support

Advantages	Disadvantages
• employees will be specialists in their jobs • tasks will be completed more quickly and to a higher standard • other employees are able to continue with their own work • noisy equipment is kept in one area	• there may be times when there is too much work and this has to be returned to departments • equipment failure will cause delays • a centralised location may be inconvenient for employees if it is far away from their own department

In many organisations there is a combination of a centralised and departmental system in operation.

Test your progress

Use the questions to test your progress.

1. Below is the organisation chart of Wacky Words plc.

a) State the job title of the person with overall responsibility for the firm.

....

b) Megan Scott needs help with a sales problem. Antony Higgins is off sick. To whom should she go to for advice?

....

c) Describe a task carried out by Amy South, Personnel Manager, on a regular basis.

....

2. What is meant by the term 'chain of command'?

....

3. Suggest one way in which an organisation chart may be helpful to new employees.

....

4. Complete the following table on tall management structure.

Advantages	Disadvantages

5. Why might an organisation restructure?

....

6. What are the benefits and problems associated with restructuring?

   a) Benefits...

....

   b) Problems..

....

7. How could administrative support assist the Personnel Department of a large organisation?

....

8. What is the name of the document given to a new employee once they have started work?

....

9. Explain the purpose of a job description.

....

10. An organisation decides to network all its computers. Which department would be responsible for the installation/maintenance of this network?

....

11. Describe a task that could be carried out by a Sales Department using a:

   a) Word processor...

   b) Database..

   c) Spreadsheet...

12. Give one advantage and one disadvantage of centralising the administrative support function.

....

....

CREDIT

Answers

1. a) Chief Executive.

   b) Martine Mitchell.

   c) Report to the Chief Executive on issues relating to the Personnel Department; responsibility for overseeing employees within the Personnel Department; interviewing applicants; etc.

2. Passing down of instructions within an organisation

3. Helps new employees learn about the organisation and the type of work it does; shows reporting structure; shows chain of command, etc.

4. Advantages: narrow span of control may make it easier for managers to supervise staff; many opportunities for promotion; may lead to motivated employees who understand their very specific roles and responsibilities. Disadvantages: employees may not feel involved in decisions made by top management; employees may not get the opportunity to show initiative; costly to have many highly paid management positions

5. Growth of organisation/its product range/numbers may require additional staff; to reduce costs the number of staff employed may be reduced (downsizing); removal of some layers of management posts (delayering) to reduce management costs; to benefit from specialists/reduce costs of employing own specialist staff, an organisation may outsource/buy in the services of another company

6. a) Benefits: Reduced (staffing) costs; improved efficiency; outsourcing may result in tasks being done quickly and to a higher standard; improved motivation.

   b) Problems: Low staff morale; resistance to change; initial communication problems; costs of restructuring

7. Word processing letters to successful/unsuccessful applicants; filing application forms, updating and maintaining employee records

8. Contract of Employment

9. Provides applicant with information about the job – job title, salary, working conditions

10. Computer Services/IT Support Department

11. a) Used to key in quotations/price lists, prepare advertising leaflets/posters;

   b) Used to store customer records;

   c) Used to record sales figures

12. Advantages: employees are specialists; tasks will be done more quickly and to a higher standard; other employees can continue with their own work; noisy equipment is kept in one area. Disadvantages: if there is too much work then tasks may need to be returned to departments; equipment failure will cause delays; wasted time as employees take tasks between departments

Office layout 1

There are two main types of office layout:
- **cellular/traditional/enclosed**
- **open plan/landscaped/flexible.**

Cellular office environment

This is a traditional method of organising the workspace where each individual employee works on their own or with a few other employees within a room.

Advantages
- Enclosed offices allow privacy for confidential meetings
- There are fewer distractions from colleagues
- Noisy equipment can be put into a separate room
- Rooms can be locked to restrict unauthorised access

Disadvantages
- Employees often feel isolated from other colleagues
- Employees may feel that they are not part of a team
- It may be difficult to supervise employees who are all working in separate rooms
- Time may be wasted with work having to be passed from room to room

Top Tip
Exam questions at Foundation/General levels may ask you to identify a layout from a graphic.

Open plan office environment

This is a modern method of organising the workspace where a large number of employees work together within the same large area.

Advantages

- Team working may be encouraged – resulting in employees who are happier and more motivated
- It is easier to supervise employees as they can all be seen
- Equipment may be shared which saves the organisation money
- Less space is wasted as there are fewer doors and walls

Disadvantages

- There is a lack of privacy for confidential meetings
- There may be many distractions – from other employees or noisy equipment
- It is difficult to restrict unauthorised access to personal belongings and confidential information
- Heating and lighting may not suit all employees

Top Tip
Exam questions regularly ask for two advantages and/or two disadvantages of one type of layout.

Factors which affect layout

An organisation will choose one type of layout depending on:
- the number of employees within the organisation
- whether the organisation will grow in size or get smaller
- the type of work/activities carried out by the organisation
- the amount of money available.

The organisation's chosen layout should:
- be adaptable to meet changes in the organisational work
- provide adequate storage
- allow employees to move around easily
- provide safe and easy access to equipment/sockets, etc.
- provide security for personal belongings and information.

Many organisations operate with an open plan layout but make private rooms available for confidential meetings.

Quick Test

1. What type of office layout is most suited to confidential work?
2. What type of office layout encourages team working?
3. Give two advantages and two disadvantages of a cellular office layout.
4. Give two advantages and two disadvantages of a open plan office layout.

Answers 1. Cellular (traditional or enclosed) office layout **2.** Open plan (landscaped/flexible) office layout **3.** Advantages: privacy for confidential meetings; fewer distractions from colleagues or noisy equipment; improved security. Disadvantages: employees may feel isolated and not part of a team; difficult to supervise employees working in separate rooms; wasted time due to work having to be passed from room to room **4.** Advantages: team working may be encouraged, resulting in happier employees; easier to supervise employees as they can all be seen; shared equipment saves money; less space wasted on doors and walls. Disadvantages: lack of privacy; more distractions from employees or noisy equipment; security is harder to maintain; heating and lighting may not suit all employees

Office layout 2

Furniture

Top Tip
Ergonomics is the study of how the working environment affects the work of the employees.

An organisation should choose an appropriate layout and then also consider the type of furniture required, where to position this furniture and how to organise the workstations.

Desks

- Size and shape should suit the work/activity to be carried out
- (Lockable) drawers should be provided for storage (personal belongings)

Storage

- Should restrict unauthorised access – lockable filing cabinets/disk storage boxes
- Should prevent damage from fire/flood – metal cabinets

Chairs

- Should be adjustable to suit individual employee (to prevent health problems)
- Should meet necessary health and safety requirements (see page 26–27)

Workstations

- Are usually L-shaped to allow the employee to carry out computer work on one part of the desk and do paperwork on the other
- Are available in different shapes/sizes to allow for use in a variety of layouts

- The layout of workstations:
  - cable management system should be in use
  - should provide storage – drawers
  - should have access to telephone lines and electrical sockets
  - should have all materials for working close to hand
  - should be organised and tidy.

At Credit level you will be asked to evaluate different layouts. You should be able to describe each type of layout, identify the differences between the layouts and be able to recommend one type of layout for a given scenario. You **must** always justify your recommendations.

Organisation of office furniture and equipment

The layout of office furniture and equipment will depend on the type of activities being carried out. It should:

- make the best possible use of the space available
- be flexible to suit the changing needs of the organisation

- provide a healthy and safe working environment
- provide an attractive and pleasant working environment
- minimise noise levels
- enable restricted access where confidential work is being carried out.

Administrative and clerical work

This type of work requires:

- a large work area with space for a computer
- access to power and telephone points
- soundproof screens to provide privacy and reduce noise levels
- adequate storage.

Meetings and interviews

This type of work requires:

- an area which is separate from the main working area – a separate room to provide privacy
- large tables for paperwork
- appropriate equipment for presentations
- refreshment facilities.

ICT in the workplace

More employees are choosing to work away from the office and so working practices have changed to reflect this. Employees are able to work:

- in the office
- at home
- whilst travelling
- in hotel accommodation
- in customers'/suppliers' premises.

Employees need to use various pieces of equipment to keep in touch with their organisation while they are working outwith the employer's premises. Such equipment includes:

- **Laptop (notebook)** – a portable computer which has the appropriate software to process information
- **Computer** – a computer at home allows an employee to continue with work as if in the office and will also allow contact via e-mail
- **Mobile phone** – allows the employee to keep in contact with the organisation
- **Personal digital assistant (PDA)** – a handheld device that combines computing, telephone/fax, and networking features
- **Pager** – can be used to contact an employee who is out of the office
- **Voice mail** – allows messages to be received when the employee is unavailable to answer the telephone
- **Fax** – allows written messages to be sent and received
- **Video-conferencing** – allows employees to take part in face-to-face meetings without having to travel.

Top Tip
Remember, when answering problem solving questions, a one-word answer does NOT solve the problem.

Quick Test

1. How can an employee who is out of the office be contacted urgently?
2. Legal work would require what type of office layout? Justify your answer.

Answers 1. Mobile phone or pager **2.** Cellular office layout; it allows confidential work to be kept secure as the office can be locked; it allows private meetings with clients to take place

Working practices

Homeworking and teleworking

Top Tip
Remember to read the question carefully. Are you being asked about advantages/ disadvantages for **employee** or **employer**?

Homeworker describes any employee who does their job from their own home.

Teleworker describes any employee who does their job away from the office with the use of ICT equipment.

Employee		Employer	
Advantages to the employee	**Disadvantages to the employee**	**Advantages to the employer**	**Disadvantages to the employer**
• Money is saved on travel costs • Time is saved on travelling • Greater flexibility in arranging hours • More responsibility for managing their own time	• Miss out on the social aspect of work • Do not feel included in the decision-making process • Distractions at home may interrupt work • May lack motivation due to lack of supervision	• Less space required at organisation's premises • Absenteeism may be reduced • Employer may be able to keep staff who may otherwise have left • Happier, more productive employees	• Cost of purchasing equipment for home use • Difficult to arrange meetings • Difficult to ensure health and safety and to provide ICT help and support • Difficult to supervise staff

Hot desk/hot room/touchdown area

Employees working from home may still need to come into the office occasionally for meetings or require access to computer facilities.

A **hot desk** is a spare desk or workstation which may be booked in advance for use by any employee. Each hot desk will be equipped with a standard layout and equipment – computer and telephone.

A **carrel** is a small booth which allows more privacy and fewer distractions for employees.

A **hot room** may be booked in advance for use by any employee/s. It may be used for confidential meetings.

A **touchdown area** is often like a coffee bar with high tables and stools with computer access and is used by employees making brief visits to the organisation. They do not need to be booked in advance and are intended to be used only for short periods of time.

A **chillout area** is an area within an open plan layout which has been separated from the work area and allows employees to take a break from work.

Working hours

Flexitime allows employees to arrange their own working hours, to start work early/late and finish early/late. However, they must work a core time (hours employees are required to be at work, for example, 10 am – 2 pm). Employees are able to build up extra hours and 'bank' these to take time off at a later date.

Job share is where one full-time job is split between two people. Each person works for their agreed proportion of the working week, receiving the same proportion of the salary, holiday, etc.

Shift work is when employees work at different times of the day/night to ensure that the organisation is always open. Employees usually work a day shift (morning and afternoon), back shift (afternoon and evening) or night shift (during the night).

Top Tip
Do not use the word **share** when defining job share or **shift** when defining shift work.

Implications of changes to working conditions

For any proposed changes to the working environment or working practices, management should consider the following issues:

- **Health and safety** – any changes in the layout must meet legal requirements (see page 26–27)
- **Staff welfare** – any change to working conditions should be as a result of consultation with employees; appropriate training must be provided
- **Managing change** – a time of change can be stressful for employees and therefore management must make sure that there is good communication; poor management of change may lead to increased absenteeism and lower productivity
- **Cost** – management should ensure that they consider the financial cost of moving to new premises, purchasing new equipment and furniture, and providing training.

Quick Test

1. Give two advantages of teleworking to an employee.

2. What does 'job share' mean?

Answers 1. Less travel saves time and money; greater flexibility in arranging hours; **2.** A full-time job which is split between two people – tasks, salary, hours, holidays

Maintaining a safe working environment

Accident prevention

Type of accident	Maintaining a safe working environment	
	Employees should:	*Employers should:*
Trip, slip, fall (from trailing cables, open filing cabinet drawers, etc.)	• never leave anything lying around that others could fall over • keep work areas tidy • avoid storing materials in a hard-to-reach place • mop up any spilled liquids immediately • be familiar with all health and safety regulations	• provide adequate storage • ensure a cable management system is in place • position furniture and equipment appropriately • provide appropriate equipment
Fire (from unsafe storage of liquids, overloaded power points, etc.)	• ensure liquids are kept away from computer equipment • never overload power sockets • report any faulty equipment immediately • never block fire exits • never smoke in unauthorised areas	• ensure fire exits are not blocked • remind staff to follow fire procedures • ensure employees are aware of organisation's no-smoking policy • maintain equipment on regular basis • have regular fire drills

Reporting of accidents and hazards

First aid

Employers must:

- ensure that an 'appointed' person is available to take charge of first-aid arrangements when someone is injured or falls ill
- ensure that a first-aider is designated
- ensure that a suitably stocked first-aid box is available
- ensure that a record is kept of all incidents
- inform all employees about first aid arrangements (names and locations of appointed persons and first-aiders, and location of first-aid box)

If an employee witnesses an accident they should:

- contact one of the organisation's first-aiders
- reassure the injured person
- wait with the injured person until the first-aider arrives
- complete an **Accident Report Form** and an **Accident Book**.

Reporting accidents

The **Accident Report Form** usually contains the following information:

- name of injured person
- position of injured person in organisation
- brief description of accident
- details of injury
- if injured person was taken to hospital/doctor
- signature of person reporting accident (can be witness or person involved in accident)
- date of birth of injured person
- date and time of accident
- place of accident
- first-aid treatment given (if any)
- name(s) and position(s) of person(s) present when accident occurred
- date of completion of report.

The **Accident Book** is a summary of all accidents which occur within the organisation. It usually contains the following information:

- date of accident
- location of accident
- name of witness
- time of accident
- name of injured person
- details of accident and action taken.

Reporting faulty equipment

Before using any equipment an employee should receive training and be authorised to use the equipment.

If an employee is using a piece of equipment which develops a fault he/she should:

- switch off equipment and pull the plug out of the socket
- place a notice on the equipment to warn others not to use the equipment
- report the fault to his/her supervisor or maintenance personnel
- complete a **Hazard/Fault Report**.

The **Hazard/Fault Report** usually contains the following information:

- location of equipment
- description of hazard/fault
- name of person reporting hazard
- signature of supervisor
- serial number of equipment/description of equipment
- action taken
- date hazard reported.

CREDIT

It is important that the correct procedure is followed when reporting a hazard. This ensures the safety of all employees, reduces the amount of time equipment is out of action and reducing the amount of work done by the organisation.

The Accident Report Form, Accident Book and Hazard/Fault Report could be stored on the organisation's network. This allows employees to access it, complete it and e-mail it immediately to the relevant person.

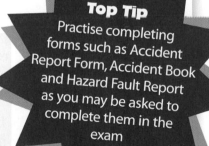

Top Tip
Practise completing forms such as Accident Report Form, Accident Book and Hazard Fault Report as you may be asked to complete them in the exam

---

Quick Test

1. What procedure should be followed if a piece of equipment develops a fault?
2. Why might it be useful to store the organisation's Accident Report Form, Accident Book and Hazard/Fault Report on a network?

Answers 1. Switch off equipment, pull the plug out of socket; place warning notice on equipment; report fault to supervisor/maintenance personnel; complete Hazard/Fault Report **2.** Allows employee to quickly complete form and e-mail it to relevant person

Health and safety legislation

Health and Safety at Work Act 1974

Employers must:

- provide a safe entrance and exit from work
- ensure safe methods of working
- ensure all employees receive clear instructions, appropriate training and adequate supervision
- ensure safe working conditions
- ensure equipment is safe and properly stored
- arrange for the safe use, storage and movement of hazardous materials
- provide protective clothing where necessary
- provide information and training on health and safety
- allow the appointment of a health and safety representative.

Employees must:

- take reasonable care of their own health and safety and the health and safety of others
- cooperate with the employer on health and safety matters
- not misuse or interfere with anything provided for employees' health and safety.

Top Tip

Exam questions often ask you to state some responsibilities of employers and employees for health and safety in general and for health and safety related to ICT.

Health and Safety (Display Screen Equipment) Regulations 1992

This Act relates to the responsibilities of employers and employees with regard to the use of ICT within the organisation.

Employers must:

- assess each individual's hardware and environment to identify potential risks; if risk is identified, steps must be taken to reduce this risk
- ensure workstations meet minimum requirements, for example, adjustable brightness/contrast controls
- arrange eye tests and provide spectacles if necessary
- provide health and safety training for employees
- organise the daily work of visual display unit (VDU) users so that there are regular rest breaks or changes in activity.

Employees must avoid potential health hazards by:

- making full use of adjustment facilities for the VDU

- arranging desk and screen to avoid glare
- not sitting for long periods of time in the same position.

The following health and safety problems are often associated with the use of display screen equipment.

Problem	Solved by
Eye strain, headaches	• Use of anti-glare screen • Repositioning VDU away from direct sunlight • Use of blinds to prevent glare • Ensuring operator has regular breaks or changes in activity • Arranging eye tests and providing spectacles if necessary
Repetitive strain injury (RSI)	• Use of wrist rests • Ensuring operator has regular breaks or changes in activity • Adjusting the layout of the workstation
Backache	• Use of **adjustable** chair • Ensuring operator has **regular** breaks or changes in activity
Stress	• Monitoring operator workload • Checking operator has been fully trained in the use of hardware and software

Workplace (Health, Safety and Welfare) Regulations 1992

These cover a wide range of basic health, safety and welfare issues such as ventilation, heating, lighting, workstations, seating and welfare facilities.

Teleworkers

Teleworkers are covered by health and safety law. Employers must provide teleworkers with safe and appropriate equipment and furniture for use in the home. They must also ensure that teleworkers receive proper training in the use of equipment.

Emergency and evacuation procedures

All workplaces require, by law, a fire certificate before they can operate as a place of business. There must also be a proper fire alarm system and a fire escape for all employees. Regular fire drills should take place to ensure staff know the sound of the alarm and the correct evacuation procedure to follow.

Fire evacuation notices (what to do in the event of a fire) should be displayed prominently for all employees and visitors to see – they should be displayed in all areas including the reception area. Staff and visitors must always sign in and out of the staff in/out book or visitor's book so that in the event of a fire all employees and visitors can be accounted for.

Reception services 1

Reception area

The receptionist is the first person a visitor will meet at an organisation. A good first impression may encourage repeat custom, increase the success of the organisation, and impress job applicants.

Layout of the reception area

The reception area should be located near the main entrance of the organisation.

A receptionist will require a large desk which should be kept neat and tidy. An organisation chart may be displayed. The waiting area should be well decorated and furnished with comfortable seats, coffee table, good lighting, pictures, plants, certificates, etc. Visitors should have access to reading material (organisational literature or magazines), refreshments and toilet facilities.

ICT in the reception area

- Computer – to allow receptionist to access electronic diary
- Fax – to deal with incoming/outgoing mail
- Telephone/answering machine/voicemail/switchboard/ mobile phone/pager – to allow receptionist to deal with incoming phone calls/customer enquiries and to allow receptionist to contact members of staff (who are in and out of the office)

Qualities and duties of a receptionist

There are a number of qualities which are considered essential for a good receptionist. When a vacancy is advertised some of these may appear in the advertisement along with a description of duties.

A good receptionist should be:

- friendly and helpful
- calm and patient
- polite
- well presented – neat and tidy in appearance
- tactful and discreet
- skilled in communicating with others
- well organised
- knowledgeable about the organisation.

A receptionist's duties include:

- greeting visitors
- making/updating appointments
- maintaining the visitors' book and the staff in/out book
- issuing visitors' passes
- directing visitors
- taking and passing on messages
- signing for incoming mail/parcels
- keeping reception area tidy
- routine duties – operating switchboard, dealing with mail, word processing, filing.

Record keeping

Top Tip
Record keeping by the receptionist may be carried out manually or electronically.

Staff in/out book

The receptionist needs to know which members of staff are in the building or when they are due back for dealing with appointments/customer enquiries. All members of staff must complete the **Staff in/out book** whenever they leave and return to the building.

Visitors' book

The receptionist must ensure that all visitors sign in the **Visitors' book** (also known as the **Reception register**) when they arrive and sign out when they leave the building. This allows the receptionist to know who is in the building in the event of an emergency evacuation.

Appointments book/electronic diary

Whenever the receptionist makes an appointment they must check that relevant staff members will be available. All appointments must be written accurately – correct date/time, name of person to be seen, name of visitor, etc.

Many organisations have computerised appointments systems. This allows appointments to be made and information to be shared with others (if on a network). The benefits of using an electronic diary include:

- appointments cannot be double-booked
- regular meetings need only be entered once
- staff details can be stored in the address book
- alerts can be used to remind the user of an appointment
- a 'to do list' may be generated
- diaries of several people can be checked to find a suitable date/time for a meeting.

Quick Test

1. Describe two features of a reception area.
2. Name two qualities of a good receptionist.
3. Describe two duties of a receptionist.
4. Give two benefits of using a computerised appointment system.

Answers 1. Located near the main entrance, well decorated, comfortable chairs, coffee table, refreshments, organisation chart, reading materials **2.** Friendly and helpful; calm and patient; see list on page 28 for other possible answers **3.** Greeting visitors to the organisation; making/updating appointments; see list on page 29 for other possible answers **4.** Appointments cannot be double-booked; regular meetings need only be entered once; see list on page 29 for other possible answers

Reception services 2

Procedure for dealing with visitors

Greet the visitor	Ask the visitor for their name, job title and organisation	Ask the visitor for the name of the person they wish to see	Ask the visitor if they have an appointment

With appointment	Without appointment
Check the appointments book/electronic diary	Contact the staff member the visitor wishes to see and ask if they can meet the visitor
Ensure the visitors' book is signed and issue a visitors' pass	
Contact relevant staff to inform them of the visitor's arrival	If the staff member is available, ensure the visitors' book is signed, issue a visitors' pass and direct the visitor to the appropriate office
If staff member is not ready to receive visitor, direct visitor to waiting area, offer refreshments	
Direct visitor to the appropriate office or wait for staff member to attend visitor in reception	If the staff member is unavailable, ask if someone else could help, and/or offer to make an appointment for another time

Security at reception

Security within any organisation is a major issue and the role of the receptionist is crucial.

It is important the there is always a member of staff at reception – relief staff should be available to cover for breaks, illness, etc. A poor impression is created if there is no-one at reception when a visitor arrives.

Security measures used within any organisation may include:

- **Appointments book/Visitors' book/Staff in and out book** – these records provide information on appointments and details on visitors and staff entering and leaving the building
- **Visitors' badges** – these are issued to visitors and allows authorised visitors to be identified by staff
- **Staff ID badges/security passes** – these allow members of staff to be easily identified – they may include a photograph as well as name, job title, department, and may need to be shown on arrival at work
- **Locked doors** – only authorised members of staff will hold a key and therefore access is restricted

Top Tip
Remember CCTV cannot stop someone from entering a room or building or from stealing personal belongings.

- **Key pad/combination locks/swipe cards** – access is restricted to those who are authorised and who have the appropriate number/plastic card
- **Entryphone** – anyone wanting to enter must contact the receptionist by buzzer/intercom before the door is opened
- **Closed circuit television (CCTV)** – this allows areas within or outside a building to be observed and recorded.

Dealing with security problems

The receptionist may have to deal with a range of security problems.

If a **suspicious parcel** is left at reception:

- never attempt to move or open the parcel – to prevent injury
- try to identify who the parcel is for and where it came from – the recipient or owner may be able to provide information about the contents of the parcel
- inform security/manager/police – they are trained to deal with this type of situation
- evacuate the building – to prevent injury
- enter the details in an **Incident book** – to provide a record of the incident.

If a **visitor is aggressive**:

- try to calm the visitor – to prevent injury
- contact security/manager – they are trained to deal with this type of situation
- inform the visitor's organisation about their behaviour – they will be able to discipline the visitor to ensure it doesn't happen again
- enter the details in an Incident book – to provide a record of the incident.

If members of staff arrive without their ID pass:

- contact their line manager – to verify the person's identity
- have photos of all staff members on file – to allow identification of the person
- remind staff of the importance of wearing ID badges and issue a daily/visitors' pass – so member of staff can start work without delay.

Top Tip

Remember – problems at Credit level require justification as well as recommendations.

Quick Test

1. Why should someone always be available at reception?
2. Name one way of restricting access to authorised personnel.
3. What should be done in the event of a suspicious parcel being found at reception?

Answers 1. It creates a poor impression of the organisation if reception is unattended. **2.** Locking doors, using key pads, combination locks, swipe cards **3.** Never attempt to move or open the parcel; try to identify who the parcel is for and where it came from; inform security/manager/police; evacuate the building; enter the details in an Incident book

Mail handling 1

Mail handling

Internal mail is communication sent and received **within** an organisation. It may be within the one building or between branches of the same organisation.

External mail is communication sent **outwith** an organisation or received from **outwith** the organisation, for example, letters to customers or from suppliers, etc.

Incoming mail

Top Tip
In a small organisation with a low volume of mail, the receptionist often deals with the mail. Large organisations are likely to have a separate mail department.

Incoming mail could be received by:

- post person (1st or 2nd class, or Special Delivery – which must be signed for on delivery)
- courier (particularly for large, bulky parcels or urgent/ valuable deliveries)
- private box (or PO box)
- e-mail
- fax
- voicemail.

- Incoming mail should be delivered to staff workstations as soon as reasonably possible.
  - This ensures that all mail is received quickly, allowing staff to complete tasks on time; it also reduces time wasted waiting for important information.

- Mail should be distributed at regular times throughout the day.
  - This allows staff to plan their tasks around when they will receive mail and important documents.

Alternatively, mail may be scanned onto the computer system, where it can either be e-mailed to relevant staff or stored and accessed on the organisation's network. Private or confidential mail would not be scanned but taken directly to the appropriate member of staff.

E-mail (electronic mail) is information sent and received via computer. It can be internal (messages sent from one computer to another within the organisation) or external (sent outwith the organisation).

Features of e-mail

- Files can be attached (spreadsheet, word processing documents, etc.)
- Priority of message can be shown (high, low)
- Important messages can be 'flagged' to remind the recipient they contain information which has to be followed up
- Groups can be created, allowing a message to be sent to all the people in a group at the same time
- A sender can use the Receipt/Confirmation facility so they know that their message has been opened
- An Out-of-office facility can be used to advise a sender if a recipient is unavailable.

Advantages of e-mail

- Communication is more efficient as information can be sent, received and acted upon quickly
- Information can be sent confidentially as passwords are required to open 'mailbox'
- Lengthy documents can be sent at low cost (as an attachment)
- Efficient communication, as one message can be sent to whole group

Disadvantages of e-mail

- Sender must know the e-mail address of the recipient
- Unless sender requests a 'Read Receipt' there is no way of knowing if recipient has opened mail
- Requires regular checking
- Problems with connection to the internet service provider can create problems

A **fax** (facsimile) is an exact copy of a document sent from one fax machine to another (this can include text, photographs and graphics). Some computers/printers can also receive/send faxes.

Fax machines are often located in the reception area, so they should **not** be used to send or receive **confidential** information.

Advantages of fax

- Speed of transmission makes it suitable for sending **urgent** information
- Relatively low cost of transmitting information

Disadvantages of fax

- May take time to reach the intended recipient (particularly if fax machine is located centrally)
- Sometimes faxed documents are not accepted as legally binding

Voicemail is a facility that lets a telephone caller leave a recorded message for an intended recipient. It is useful for when a staff member is out of the office, unavailable or already on the telephone. It enables the staff member to handle queries as soon as they are available and means the customer doesn't have to call back.

Equipment used for incoming mail

- Date stamp – used to place date of arrival on mail (useful if there is a query about when document was received)
- Photocopier – to make additional copies of letters which have to be seen by more than one person
- Fax (see above)
- Scanner (see page 32)

Quick Test

1. Define the term 'internal mail'.
2. Give an example of when voicemail could be used.
3. State two pieces of equipment used for incoming mail.
4. Why is it important that mail be delivered before staff begin work?

Answers 1. Communication sent and received within an organisation **2.** When member of staff is unavailable to take phone call **3.** Date stamp; photocopier; fax; scanner **4.** Allows staff to complete tasks, reduces time wasting

Mail handling 2

Outgoing mail

Outgoing mail should be collected from departments at regular intervals throughout the day.

This spreads the workload of the mailroom staff. It also means that staff do not need to interrupt their work and leave their workstation to take post to mailroom.

Mail will be sorted by mailroom staff into categories (first or second class, parcels, courier, Special Delivery, etc.) and postal charges will be calculated (based on size, weight and thickness of the package, and method of delivery). Mail is then **franked** with the correct value or stamps to the correct value could be placed on the package. Alternatively postage could be purchased online, printed in the office and placed on the package.

Top Tip
Large organisations may use Royal Mail Business Collection service where the Royal Mail will come to the organisation's premises to collect all outgoing mail.

Equipment used for outgoing mail

- Franking machine – prints a postal impression in red onto envelopes or labels. Postage is purchased from the Post Office in advance and the machine can be topped up with any amount by telephoning the Post Office.
- Postal scales – used to weigh packages to calculate postage. Can be electronic or manual.

Other equipment which may be used in the preparation of outgoing mail include addressing machines, folding and inserting machines and labelling machines. Fax and e-mail are also used to send outgoing mail.

Methods of sending mail

First and second class post – these are used for sending **non-urgent**, **routine** information. First class mail aims to deliver the letter or packet the next working day, whereas second class aims to deliver letters or packets by the third working day, however, these are not guaranteed.

Courier – this is appropriate for sending **bulky parcels**, **legal documents** or **urgent** or **valuable** information. Delivery time is usually guaranteed – it can even be same-day delivery. Private firms and Royal Mail provide this service.

Recorded signed for – this is used for sending **important** documents (for example, legal documents, job application forms), when the sender wants proof/confirmation of delivery. Most first class recorded items are delivered the next working day (but this is not guaranteed).

Special Delivery – this is used for sending **urgent** or **valuable** mail. *Special Delivery 9.00 am* guarantees that mail will be delivered by 9 am the following day. *Special Delivery Next day* guarantees that mail will be delivered the next day before 1 pm. Proof of posting, signature on arrival, online confirmation of delivery as well as compensation if mail goes missing is available.

Benefits of sending mail by post and electronically

Post

- Actual documents can be sent
- Bulky items can be sent
- Some organisation's customers may not have e-mail or fax facilities
- When original documents are required (so cannot be sent electronically), such as passport, driver's licence, legal documents

Electronically (e-mail, fax)

- Suitable for urgent information as delivery/transmission is immediate
- Information can be sent at a time convenient to sender (available 24 hours per day)
- Allows for an immediate reply
- Relatively cheap

Appropriate methods of sending information

You should be able to suggest the most appropriate methods of sending information. To help you, some examples are shown in the table below.

You also need to justify your suggestion and say why you think this is the best method.

Type of communication	Suggested method(s)	Justification
Legal contract	Courier or post – possibly Special Delivery or Recorded signed for	Original documents are required
Confirmation of hotel booking tonight	Fax or e-mail	Information is required immediately
Box of sales catalogues to arrive in Manchester tomorrow	Courier	Bulky items required urgently
Letters to customers inviting them to sales event next week	Post (first or second class)	Not all customers will have access to e-mail or fax; not urgent
Information to all employees	Intranet, e-mail, posters	Ensures all employees can access information
Employee database file required by personnel immediately	E-mail (with attachment)	Attachment can be edited; confidential information can be sent by e-mail

Quick Test

1. Why should outgoing mail be collected at regular intervals?
2. What type of information would be sent by first/second class post?
3. State two pieces of equipment used in the preparation of outgoing mail.
4. Why should a box of catalogues be sent by courier?

Answers 1. Spread work of mailroom staff; saves staff wasting time taking mail to mailroom **2.** Non-urgent, routine items **3.** Franking machine; postal scales **4.** It is bulky

Test your progress

Use the questions to test your progress.

1. Name and describe two features of an open plan office layout which can be used to provide fewer distractions for employees.

   ....

   ....

2. Explain what is meant by the following terms.

   a) Flexitime...

   b) Job sharing..

   c) Teleworking..

3. Explain how ICT can be used in flexible working practices.

   ....

   ....

4. Employers and employees have a responsibility to maintain a safe working environment. State two ways in which employers and employees can maintain a safe working environment.

   a) Employers..

   ....

   ....

   b) Employees..

   ....

   ....

5. The following health and safety problems have been identified at Hamilton Printers. Give a solution for each problem described.
   a) No record of any accidents is kept.

   ....

   ....

   b) Computer operators regularly complain of backache.

   ....

   ....

   c) The receptionist injured herself falling over trailing wires.

   ....

   ....

   d) Staff and visitors were unsure of fire evacuation procedures at a recent fire drill.

   ....

   ....

6. Describe the purpose of the following.

   a) Staff in/out book...

   b) Reception register...

7. Describe two benefits of using an electronic diary.

....

....

8. Describe three features of e-mail.

....

....

9. State when it would be most appropriate to use the following methods of sending mail (the first one has been done for you).

a) Fax *used for urgent, non-confidential mail*

b) E-mail...

c) Recorded signed for...

CREDIT

10. Justify the use of an anti-glare screen to prevent headaches.

....

....

11. How does a receptionist assist with security in an organisation?

....

....

12. State and justify how the following information should be sent.

a) Confirmation of a hotel booking for tonight...

....

....

b) Employee database urgently required by Personnel Department.........................

....

....

Answers

1. Carrel – a small booth; dividers/plants – to section part of the office off

2. **a)** Employees arrange their own working hours based around a core time;
   b) One full-time job split between two people; sharing hours, working conditions, pay;

3. **c)** Working away from the office (usually at home) using ICT equipment
   Laptop – portable, with appropriate software that allows employee to process/access information available when away from the office. Home computer – allows employee to continue to work as if in the office. Mobile phone – allows employee to keep in contact with the organisation

4. **a)** Provide adequate storage areas; ensure a cable management system is in place, etc. b) Should never leave anything lying around that others could fall over; keep work areas tidy and free from hazards; ensure familiarity with all health and safety regulations; report any faulty equipment immediately, etc.

5. **a)** Accident report forms and an Accident book should be maintained;
   b) Provide computer operators with an adjustable chair/regular breaks;
   c) Install a cable management system;
   d) Place fire evacuation procedure notices in the reception area/train staff to help visitors

6. **a)** So receptionist knows which members of staff are in the building to deal with appointments/enquiries;
   b) So receptionist knows who is in the building in the event of an emergency evacuation

7. Appointments cannot be double-booked; regular meetings need be entered only once; staff details can be stored in the address book, etc.

8. Files can be inserted and sent as an attachment; priority of message can be shown; important messages can be flagged to remind recipient they contain information to be followed up, etc.

9. **b)** Used for urgent, confidential information;
   c) Used for sending important documents

10. Prevents glare on screen which can cause headaches

11. Keeps appointments book/visitors' book, staff in/out book; issues visitors' badges/staff ID badges/security passes; uses entryphone, CCTV, etc.

12. **a)** E-mail or fax as the information must be received immediately and taken with employee going on trip;
    b) E-mail as database can be attached for editing and sent/received immediately

Filing

Purpose of filing

Filing is the process of storing documents in an appropriate, easily accessible way. Documents are filed for the following reasons:

- to **find** information quickly when it is required
- to keep documents **secure** (particularly confidential information)
- to keep documents in **good condition**
- to satisfy **legal requirements**, for example, organisations may have to keep bank statements for a number of years.

Filing can be done **manually** or **electronically**.

Features of a good filing system

A filing system (whether manual or electronic) should be:

- **secure** (lockable) – so confidential information can be stored safely
- **conveniently located** – it must be decided whether centralised/departmental/electronic filing is more appropriate
- **safe**, for example, fire proof
- **flexible** – to meet the changing needs of the organisation, for example, it should be able to expand if necessary
- **appropriate** for the type of information held
- **quick** and **simple** to use
- **economical** in terms of set-up, training and running costs

It should not take up too much space.

Top Tip
A filing system may be manual or electronic.

File management

File management describes the method in which information is stored and organised. Good file management allows documents/files to be found quickly, reducing time spent searching. File management refers to documents stored both manually and electronically.

An effective file management system would include the following:

- all files have an appropriate filename (relevant to information they contain)
- all related files are stored in an appropriately named folder
- folders may be stored in a directory (if electronic filing system in use)
- all out-of-date files are deleted/removed regularly.

Quick Test

1. What is meant by the term 'filing'?
2. Why are documents filed?
3. Why is it important that an effective file management system is in operation?

Manual filing

This is a traditional method of filing where paper documents are kept in box files, lever arch folders, filing cabinets, etc.

Filing procedures

To ensure that documents/information can be found easily and quickly, it is important that basic filing procedures are followed.

- Filing should be carried out on a **regular** basis.
- When a file is removed from the filing cabinet, an **out card** (also known as **out guide** or **absent card**) should be completed and placed in the filing cabinet at the point where the file was removed; the out card should show who removed the file and the date of removal.
- A **cross-reference** card should be used where a file could be placed in more than one place in the filing cabinet.
- After a document has been used a **release mark** should be placed on the document indicating that it is ready to be filed; this mark could be 'F', an employee's initials etc.
- Old or out-of-date files should be regularly removed from the filing system – important files may be **archived** to leave space for current files. Organisations should have a policy on how long to keep particular documents etc.

Systems of classification

This refers to the way in which folders and files are arranged for storage and reference within filing cabinets.

Classification	Features	Advantages	Disadvantages
Alphabetical	Folders/files are arranged in order of the alphabet	• Easy to understand and use • Direct method of filing (an index is not required)	• Training may be required on complex rules if index is used • Expansion may be difficult – reorganisation of cabinet drawers may be needed if a letter needs more space
Numerical	Folders/files are arranged in numerical order	• Expansion is straightforward	• Requires index system (card index matching customer names to file numbers) • Transposition of file numbers may cause problems
Chronological	Folders/files arranged in date order	• Most recent correspondence is easily found	• Never used on its own; usually with another filing system

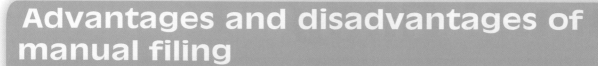

Advantages and disadvantages of manual filing

Advantages

- Easy to use – little training required
- Many people prefer to read original documents. It may be necessary to use original files, such as legal documents

Disadvantages

- Filing cabinets can take up a lot of space
- It may be time consuming to search for information if system of classification is unclear

Centralised and departmental filing

Centralised filing is when all of the organisation's documents are stored in one central location. All files are stored using the same system of classification.

Departmental filing is when each department within the organisation stores its own documents. Each department uses the system of classification which best suits its needs.

System	Advantages	Disadvantages
Centralised	• Expert filing staff are trained in filing system, so files should be found easily and efficiently • Less equipment is required, saving organisation money and space	• Time may be wasted by employees walking to collect and return files (and not doing more meaningful tasks) • The same system of classification may not suit all records within the organisation, for example, the Finance Department may prefer a numerical system of filing whereas the Human Resources Department may prefer alphabetical
Departmental	• Files and information are readily available • Method of filing is suited to the needs of individual departments	• Filing equipment is needed for every department which costs more money • Duplicates of the same files may occur when more than one department requires the same information

Quick Test

1. What should be placed in a filing cabinet when a file is removed?
2. State one advantage of alphabetical and one advantage of numerical filing.
3. Why might an organisation choose to have a centralised filing department?

Answers 1. An out card **2.** Alphabetical: easy to use, direct method of filing; Numerical: easy to expand **3.** Expertise of filing staff means files are found easily; save money on equipment; save space

Electronic filing

Electronic filing refers to the storage of documents and files on computer. To store information electronically, documents and files must first be created using a suitable software package, for example, database, spreadsheet, word processing, desktop publishing (DTP).

Information can also be scanned onto the computer system and saved using appropriate software.

Database software

A **database** is an organised collection of (related) information.

Using database software means that the information contained in the database is structured, this allows the information to be manipulated (changed) for the user's own needs eg it can be searched (filtered) to identify some common criteria.

Databases are made up of fields and records. **Fields** are the headings/names for each individual item of information, and they are the items which can be searched. Together, all the fields make up a database **record**.

Fields can be **formatted** to allow only a particular type of information to be entered. Examples of formatting include text, number, date/time, and currency.

In the example below there are six records and nine fields. The *start date* is formatted as date/time and *salary* is formatted as currency. This database has been **sorted** in alphabetical order of surname.

record　　　　　　　　　　　　　　　　　　　　　　　**fields**

EMPLOYEE DATABASE : Table

FIRST NAME	SURNAME	ADDRESS LINE 1	TOWN	POSTCODE	DEPARTMENT	JOB TITLE	START DATE	SALARY
Antony	Armstrong	32 Raven Drive	Motherwell	ML1 5EW	Purchasing	Purchasing Manager	22/06/2001	£30,000.00
Amy	Dolan	26 Glen Isla	Hamilton	ML8 7YH	Sales	Sales Manager	16/09/2004	£28,500.00
Eva	Higgins	6 Orkney Road	Glasgow	G10 2XA	Personnel	Personnel Assistant	09/10/2004	£11,500.00
Robert	Kerr	4 Cullen Lane	Wishaw	ML2 6TE	Purchasing	Purchasing Assistant	05/08/2005	£12,000.00
Niamh	McDonnell	5 Fir Lane	Glasgow	G9 4DA	Sales	Sales Assistant	10/09/2005	£11,500.00
Lewis	Smith	78 Dickson Drive	East Kilbride	G74 0OP	Personnel	Personnel Manager	28/09/2003	£25,000.00

Advantages of databases

- Records can be found quickly using the **search** facility.
- Complex searches can be carried out by **searching on two fields**, for example you could find out the names of all employees who work in the Personnel Department **and** earn more that £20,000.
- Records can be arranged into required order quickly using the **sort** facility.
- A **query** can be used to create a **report**.
- The **mailmerge** facility can be used to personalise letters.

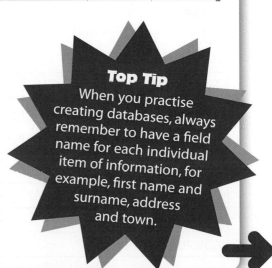

Top Tip

When you practise creating databases, always remember to have a field name for each individual item of information, for example, first name and surname, address and town.

→ ## Uses of databases

Department	Information stored
Human Resources/Personnel	Employee information; training information
Sales	Customer information
Purchases	Supplier information

Spreadsheet software

Spreadsheet software allows the user to enter numbers and text into a table with rows and columns. Formulae can be entered into the required cells which allow the spreadsheet to make automatic calculations and recalculations.

Each cell address is made up of the column letter and row number, for example, cell **E4** is highlighted above.

columns

	A	B	C	D	E
1	MONTHLY SALES FIGURES				
2					
3		January	February	March	TOTAL
4	Inverness	£9,000	£8,000	£8,500	£25,500
5	Aberdeen	£15,000	£25,000	£22,000	£62,000
6	Perth	£4,500	£6,000	£7,640	£18,140
7	Stirling	£4,900	£5,500	£4,750	£15,150
8	Dumfries	£5,000	£5,000	£5,000	£15,000
9	TOTAL	£38,400	£49,500	£47,890	£135,790

record → 4

You can replicate a formula by clicking on the black square in the bottom right side of the box and dragging down

A formula was entered into cell E4 to calculate the total sales for the Inverness branch. The formula entered was **=sum(B4:D4)**

This formula was then **replicated** (copied) into cells E5 to E9, as the same formula needed to be entered in each of these cells. If a formula is correct and replicated to appropriate cells, it reduces the chance of errors occurring and thus ensures the spreadsheet is accurate.

Formula

Type of calculation	Formula

Addition
    To add two cells together
    To add a range of cells together
	=B2+B3
	=sum(B2:B5)

Subtraction	=B2-B3
Division by 2	=B2/2
Multiplication by 2	=B2*2
Absolute formula	=B2*2

	A	B	C
1	SALES FIGURES FOR UMBRELLAS		
2			
3		Selling Price	5.99 ←
4		Units Sold	Sales
5	January	150	C3*B5
6	February	200	C3*B6
7	March	300	C3*B7
8	April	350	C3*B8
9			

An **absolute formula** was used here and replicated as we wished to calculate the sales figure using the same cell reference – the selling price.

An **absolute cell reference** is used when the formula must always refer to one specific cell. In the above example the same selling price was used to calculate sales and therefore an absolute reference was used.

Advantages of using spreadsheets

- Formulae can be entered and calculations done – if the formula is entered correctly then the spreadsheet will be accurate.
- Formulae can be replicated which saves time, especially if using a large spreadsheet.
- Changes can be made to the spreadsheet and calculations will be updated automatically.
- The spreadsheet can be sorted into required order using the sort facility.
- Charts and graphs can be produced from data in spreadsheets.

Uses of spreadsheets

Department	Used for
Finance Department	• Calculating staff wages • Calculating profit/loss figures • Preparing departmental budgets
Sales Department	• Creating graphs to show sales figures • Preparing 'What if?' scenarios, for example, 'What if the selling price changed, how would it affect overall sales?'
Purchasing Department	• Keeping stock records up to date • Completing order forms

Quick Test

1. Define the term 'database'.
2. Give two examples of how a database field could be formatted.
3. What information would the Human Resources/Personnel Department store in a database?
4. Why is it a good idea to replicate formulae in spreadsheets?
5. What would the Finance Department use a spreadsheet for?

Answers 1. A database is an organised collection of (related) information **2.** Text; date/time; numbers; currency **3.** Employee information; training information **4.** Reduces mistakes; improving accuracy of spreadsheet **5.** Calculating staff wages; calculating profit/loss figures; preparing departmental budgets

Word processing and desktop publishing software

These are used to create letters, memos, forms and newsletters. Commonly used layouts (such as letters with the company letterhead) are often stored on the intranet as templates. This ensures documents are prepared in a consistent way. It makes it easier for new staff to learn layouts and it gives customers an impression of professionalism.

When the same layout is used for the same type of document it is known as the **house style** layout.

Integrated software packages combine several applications in the one computer program, typically word processing, database, spreadsheet, graphics and communications; Microsoft Office and Appleworks are examples. There are many advantages of integrated software packages:

- The human computer interface (the on-screen layouts and instructions) are similar in the applications, making it easier to learn and use all applications.

- Data is easily transferred between applications – a chart created on a spreadsheet can be imported into a word processing application.

- Mailmerge can be carried out – information in the database can be linked to the word processing application to personalise letters.

- Dynamic linkage is possible – changes made to data in one application (e.g. spreadsheet) can be made automatically to appropriate data in another application (chart in letter created in word processing package).

- An integrated package may be cheaper than buying software packages individually.

Storage media

- The amount of storage on a **hard drive** is measured in gigabytes (Gb). The amount required by an individual will depend on the applications they use and the amount of data to be stored.

- A **floppy disk** can be used to store and transfer files between different computers. More reliable and space efficient methods of storing data are now more common.

- A **zip disk** has greater storage capacity than a floppy disk, which means it can store larger files.

- A **CD-Rom** has a large storage capacity (about 740 Mb), so many reference sources, such as encyclopedias, are provided in this format. Application packages are often distributed on CD-Rom, which is used to install the application on the computer's hard drive.

- A **DVD** (digital versatile disk or digital video disk) looks similar to a CD-Rom but has much greater storage capacity (enough to store a full-length movie).

- A **removable flash memory** card (stick, pen drive) is like a portable disk drive, small enough to be carried on a key ring. It is plugged into the computer's USB port and allows data to be transferred easily from one machine to another.

Advantages and disadvantages of electronic filing

Advantages

- Takes up less space than a manual filing system
- Documents/files/information can be located quickly using search criteria
- Multi-user access is possible (where computers are networked)
- Remote user access is possible – an employee can access files away from the office
- Back-up files can be made
- Passwords can be used to restrict access to confidential information

Disadvantages

- Initial cost of hardware and software may be high
- Cost of training employees on how to use equipment/software may be high
- Compliance with Data Protection Act is necessary (see page 49)
- If the computer system develops a fault it may be difficult to retrieve information when required

Top Tip
You should also be aware of health and safety implications for operators who use computers for a significant part of their day

Evaluation of filing methods

The following factors should be considered when deciding whether to set up a manual or electronic filing system. Note: security should also be considered (see pages 46–49).

Factor	Manual	Electronic
Cost	• Type of filing equipment required (and therefore cost) will depend on type of documents to be stored • Number of filing cabinets required will depend on whether centralised filing or departmental filing is used	• Equipment – installation and maintenance • Training costs • Security costs
Space	• Is there enough space for vertical filing cabinets? • Will expansion cause a problem?	• Lockable cabinets required for back-up storage
Training	• Filing staff may need to be trained in the use of indexing rules (depending on system of classification used)	• Training on hardware and software

Quick Test

1. Why might an organisation follow a house style layout when preparing documents?

2. Name three types of storage media.

3. What is meant by the term 'integrated software package'?

4. What three factors should be considered before deciding to set up a manual or electronic filing system?

Security of information 1

Managing user access

Data held on computer may be damaged or destroyed, accidentally or otherwise in the following ways:

- The computer **crashes** – this could be caused by an electrical fault or a problem inside the computer.
- The computer itself may be **stolen** (any data stored on the hard drive is therefore also stolen).
- Staff who are not trained in the use of the equipment/software may **accidentally delete** files.
- Hackers (people who access data without permission) may **deliberately edit or delete** data.
- **Fraud** – where employees deliberately edit or delete data for their own purposes.

Computers and data can be protected in the following ways:

- Computers can be **locked** in a room accessed only by authorised members of staff.
- Computers may be **password protected**.
- Files may be **password protected**.
- Files can be saved as **read only** documents so they cannot be changed by other users.
- **Security ID cards/keys** which are inserted into the computer restrict access.
- Other **security devices** used to restrict access include voiceprint and fingerprint recognition, and iris (eye)/signature scanners.
- **Anti-virus software** should be installed to ensure that no computer virus can corrupt the data. Viruses are computer programs which are transferred from computer to computer through the use of infected disks, e-mail and intranet/internet. A virus may delete everything on the computer or slow down the working of the computer. Regularly scanning the computer or using anti-virus software which automatically scans any input will prevent this. Anti-virus software must be updated regularly.
- All staff should be regularly reminded not to use personal disks or use e-mail facilities for personal use.

Top Tip
Remember – computers/data can be protected physically by locking computer/data away or electronically by using passwords.

When a computer user leaves their workstation at any time they must be careful to take appropriate steps to restrict access to unauthorised users, such as:

- save and close the file
- follow a shut-down procedure
- activate a password-protected screen saver
- remove data storage medium and lock away.

Screens should always be positioned away from the view of passing members of the public or visitors so they cannot be read by unauthorised personnel.

Computer printouts should never be left lying around – they should be filed or shredded.

Quick Test

1. Give two examples of how computer data can be damaged or destroyed.

2. What is a computer virus?

3. Why should employees not use e-mail for personal use?

4. What should a computer user do when they leave their workstation to go for lunch?

Answers 1. Computer may crash or be stolen; data may be edited or deleted by employees through lack of training; hackers; fraudulent use by employees **2.** A computer program designed to deliberately corrupt files or wipe the entire contents of the hard disk **3.** They could open a file attachment containing a virus and infect the organisation's computer/network **4.** Save and close file; shut down; activate password-protected screensaver; remove data storage medium and lock away

Security of information 2

Passwords

Organisations must protect the data which is stored on computer. This can be done by giving staff members **passwords** which restrict unauthorised access to files and computers.

- Restrict access to **computers** – the computer can be used only when the username/password is entered correctly.
- Restrict access to **files** – in order to open a file the user must enter the correct password. Files may have different levels of access – different passwords allow access to different amounts of data.
- Restrict access to **e-mail facilities** – this helps to ensure that any e-mail containing confidential information is accessed only by the person to whom the e-mail was addressed.

Passwords should:	Passwords should not:
<ul><li>contain a combination of letters and numbers</li><li>be changed regularly</li><li>be kept confidential.</li></ul>	<ul><li>be shared with anyone</li><li>be obvious, such as birthday, star sign, name of spouse/child/pet.</li></ul>

Passwords may also be used with a screensaver. If a user leaves their workstation, they may activate the password-controlled screensaver. This ensures that others cannot see and do not have access to the current document. The user can only return to the document by entering the correct password to stop the screensaver program.

Top Tip

'Password protection' is usually an answer to a problem solving question. Make your answer specific – password protected computer/file/screensaver/e-mail. Don't just say 'use a password'.

Care of data storage media

Data can be stored using several media – floppy disks, CDs, DVDs, and removable flash memory drives (sticks, pens, etc.). To ensure the confidentiality of the stored data, these items should be locked in a box when not in use. Floppy disks, CDs and DVDs should always be:

- labelled appropriately
- handled carefully (do not touch the metal plate on a floppy disk, or scratch/damage the CD or DVD)
- stored in covers or cases
- removed from computer when not in use
- stored away from direct sunlight.

Back-up procedures

Computer data must be backed up regularly. This means making a **second copy** of the data which is then stored **separately**. Computer data is backed up in case the original data is lost or damaged for any of the following reasons:

- the computer crashes
- fire or flood
- computer virus
- computer/data is stolen
- malicious damage to hardware/software
- accidental damage to hardware/software.

Top Tip
When asked about back-up procedures in an exam you should always state that these must be done **regularly**.

Data Protection Acts (1984, 1998)

The Data Protection Act is a law which protects the **data subject** (the person about whom information is held). It applies to data stored on computer, but not to information on paper.

All organisations (with a few exceptions, such as those dealing with national security, and the police) which hold data about individuals on computer must be registered as a **data user** with the **Data Protection Registrar** and follow the principles of the Act.

The Act describes eight main principles, which are that personal data must be:

- fairly and lawfully processed
- processed for specified purposes and not in any manner incompatible with those purposes
- adequate, relevant and not excessive
- accurate
- kept for no longer than is necessary
- processed in line with the individual's legal rights
- kept securely
- transferred to countries outside the European Economic Area, only if the individual's rights can be assured.

Failure to comply with the Data Protection Act is a criminal offence. Any organisation found to be in breach of this Act may be fined. If the data subject suffers undue stress as a result of an organisation not complying with the principles, they can sue for compensation. Data must be made available to the data subject upon request.

Quick Test

1. A file has been edited by an unauthorised employee. How could this have been prevented?

2. Explain what is meant by the term 'back-up'.

3. Describe two principles of the Data Protection Act.

4. Why must organisations comply with the Data Protection Act?

Answers 1. File should have been password protected or saved as a read only file **2.** This is a second copy of a file stored separately from the original **3.** Data must be obtained lawfully; not held for longer than necessary (see list for other answers) **4.** It is a criminal offence not to comply with the Data Protection Act; non-compliant organisations can be sued by data subject or fined

Test your progress

Use the questions to test your progress.

1. What are the features of an effective file management system?

   ....

2. State one advantage and one disadvantage of manual filing.

   ....

   ....

3. Explain the following database terms:
   a) Field..
   b) Record...
   c) Formatting a field...

4. Explain two advantages of using an electronic database.

   ....

   ....

5. When using a spreadsheet, how could a formula be placed in all relevant cells without re-keying the formula each time?

   ....

6. Explain two advantages of using a spreadsheet.

   ....

   ....

7. a) A database would be used in the Human Resources Department to store ....
      Records.
   b) A spreadsheet would be used in the Sales Department to ....

   ....

8. Give two reasons for restricting access to computer files.

   ....

   ....

9. Give two different examples of ways in which electronic data can be protected.

   ....

   ....

10. How might a virus be spread from computer to computer within an organisation?

   ....

11. Describe a back-up procedure.

....

12. What is meant by the term 'centralised filing' system?

....

13. State one advantage of centralised filing.

....

14. What are the advantages of using a 'departmental filing system'?

....

15. a) Define the term 'integrated software package'.

....

b) State two advantages of using an integrated software package.

....

....

16. Describe two provisions of the Data Protection Act.

....

....

Answers

1. All files given an appropriate filename: all related files stored in an appropriately named folder: folders stored in a directory: all out-of-date files deleted regularly

2. Advantage: little training required: many people prefer reading original documents. Disadvantage: filing cabinets can take up a lot of space: it can be time consuming to search for information if unsure of system of classification

3. a) The searchable headings/names for each individual item of information in a database:
b) Information contained in all fields:
c) Allowing only a particular type of information to be entered in that field

4. Records can be found quickly using the search facility: complex searches can be carried out by searching on two fields: records can be arranged into required order quickly using the sort facility: specific information (reports) can be created using the query facility: the mailmerge facility can be used to personalise letters

5. Replicate the formula into required cells

6. Formula can be entered and calculations done – if the formula is entered correctly then the spreadsheet will be accurate: formulae can be replicated which saves time. especially if using a large spreadsheet: if changes are made to the spreadsheet then calculations will be recalculated automatically: spreadsheet can be sorted into required order using the sort facility: charts and graphs can be produced from data in spreadsheet

7. a) Employee:
b) record sales figures

8. May contain confidential information: prevent unauthorised access to information: required under *Data Protection Act*

9. Computers may be password protected: files may be password protected: save files as 'read only' documents: restrict access to computer using security ID cards/keys or other security devices such as voiceprint/fingerprint recognition, iris (eye)/signature scanners

10. Through the use of infected disks, e-mail and intranet

11. Making a second copy to be stored separately in case data is lost

12. When all of the organisation's documents are stored in one central location and stored/filed using the same system of classification

13. Staff are trained in filing system, so should find files easily and efficiently: less equipment is required thus saving organisation money and space

14. Files and information are readily available: the method of filing is suited to the requirements of individual departments

15. a) Software that combines several applications in the one computer program. typically word processing, database, spreadsheet, graphics and communications:
b) Layouts and instructions will be similar in all applications making it easier to learn and use all applications: data can be easily transferred between applications. including automatic links and changes to data

16. Fairly and lawfully processed: processed for specified purposes and not in any manner incompatible with those purposes: adequate, relevant and not excessive: accurate: kept for no longer than is necessary: processed in line with the individual's legal rights: kept securely: transferred to countries outside the European Economic Area, only if the individual's rights can be assured

Equipment and software

Equipment and software

The process of copying documents is known as reprography. The type of equipment used will depend on the task. Very often a range of equipment will be required for a particular task.

Equipment/ Software	Description/Use	Tasks
Photocopier	• Provides an exact copy quickly • Copies can be made on to paper, card, OHP transparencies and in various sizes – A5, A4, A3 • Back-to-back copies can be made • Multi-page documents can be collated/stapled • Documents can be enlarged/reduced in size, or darkened/lightened • Colour copies can be produced • Can be linked to computer to produce copies directly from the computer	• Staff handbooks • Price lists • Policy documents, e.g. Health and Safety policy • OHP transparencies
Laminator	• Uses heat to seal documents inside a plastic coating • Document is protected from wear and tear • Documents are easily wiped clean	• Plastic cover for booklets • Posters/notices • ID passes
Binder	• Holds pages of a booklet together • Looks professional • A **comb binder** is used to punch holes along the length of the pages; a plastic comb fits into the holes and holds the pages together • A **thermal binder** uses heat to fasten an adhesive (glue) spine to hold the pages together	• Staff handbook • Reports • Instruction booklets • Organisational policies
Scanner	• A document/graphic is placed into the scanner which then transfers an exact copy to a linked computer for storage • The scanned image can be inserted into other documents or edited • Allows incoming mail to be stored on computer, e.g. application forms • To allow incoming mail to be put onto the organisational intranet	• Catalogues • Handbooks • Intranet • Incoming mail

Equipment/ Software	Description/Use	Tasks
Digital camera	• Allows photographs to be taken and downloaded onto computer for storage • Photograph can be inserted into documents or edited	• Documents requiring photos, e.g. staff manuals, property schedules
DTP/ Graphics/ Word Processing software	• Software which allows a user to create professional looking pages including text and graphics/photographs • A variety of fonts, sizes, styles can be used • Finished pages can be previewed on screen before printing	• Magazines • Sales catalogues • Posters • Forms • Organisational booklets
Inkjet printer	• Text and graphics can be printed • Can print onto different sizes of paper or card, e.g. A5, A4 and envelopes, labels, OHP transparencies • Can print in colour • Relatively portable • Inexpensive to buy (compared to laser)	• Small runs of documents • Master copies of documents to be photocopied • Posters
Laser printer	• Text and graphics can be printed • Can print onto different sizes of paper or card, e.g. A5, A4 and envelopes, labels, OHP transparencies • Can print in colour (although this is more expensive than inkjet) • Very fast and high quality • Can be expensive to buy	• Large runs of documents • Producing personalised letters to customers or suppliers

Top Tip
If you are asked to name a piece of equipment used to complete a task, saying 'computer' is not acceptable on its own.

Quick Test

1. What pieces of equipment or software may be used to produce a visitor's pass?
2. Describe one use of a scanner.
3. The staff handbook is too thick to be stapled. How could this problem be overcome?
4. An organisation produces glossy documents which include colour photographs for several hundred customers. Which type of printer would be best for this task?

Answers 1. DTP, word processing package, graphics package, printer (inkjet or laser), photocopier, laminator **2.** To allow graphics/photographs/documents/incoming mail to be stored on computer **3.** Use a binder **4.** Laser printer

Staff training

Staff training

CREDIT

Staff working within the Reprographics Department must be trained for the following reasons:

- so they know how to use the equipment safely
- so they know what to do in the event of a fault
- so they can use the equipment efficiently – producing high quality output and reducing waste
- to be familiar with appropriate legislation, such as copyright laws.

The training offered to staff should:

- reflect the level of experience and responsibilities of staff
- be carried out by a qualified trainer
- always be carried out when a new piece of equipment is installed
- consist of a practical demonstration of the equipment
- allow supervision until staff are confident in the use of the new equipment
- include dealing with minor faults/maintenance/cleaning of the equipment
- be offered to all new staff
- be updated regularly for all staff.

Top Tip
'Train them' is an inadequate answer to a Credit question – you must state what the training involves and why it is necessary.

Quick Test

1. Why do reprographics staff need training?
2. What should an organisation do to ensure that new equipment is used safely?

Answers 1. So they know how to use the equipment safely; to know what to do in the event of a fault; to be able to use the equipment efficiently; to be familiar with appropriate legislation. **2.** Train staff in the use and maintenance of equipment.

In-house and external agencies

CREDIT

Reprography may be carried out within the organisation (in-house) or by using an external agency. To carry out reprographics tasks in-house, an organisation must consider the following:

- The task to be completed
  - Does it include text, graphics, photographs?
  - Is it to be in colour?
  - The number of copies required
  - The required quality of the finished product
  - The timescale involved

- The cost of purchasing the equipment
- The running costs of the equipment
- The training of staff to use and maintain the equipment

If an organisation chooses to complete tasks using in-house staff and does not have a centralised reprographics department, then staff are not specialised and will also have other duties.

Advantages and disadvantages

Method	Advantages	Disadvantages
In-house	• Tasks can be completed quickly – no delay in sending work out and waiting for its return • In-house tasks can be prioritised and 'fed in' • Cheaper than using an external agency	• Cost of purchasing equipment is high • Staff must be trained to use equipment – costly in time and money • Equipment must be maintained
External agency	• Specialist trained staff can complete tasks very quickly and to a high standard • May be cost-effective for large volumes of tasks • Specialist equipment is available	• May be costly for small tasks • There may be difficulties in explaining the exact requirements, so delays may arise

Top Tip
An exam question may ask you to make a recommendation as to whether an organisation should choose in-house staff or external agency for a specific reprographic task. To answer this question well you should make a comparison between the two methods and justify your recommendation.

Quick Test

1. Give two advantages of copying in-house.
2. Give two reasons for choosing an external agency.

Answers 1. Tasks can be completed quickly – no delay in sending work out and waiting for its return; in-house tasks can be prioritised and 'fed in'; cheaper than using an external agency. 2. Specialist staff can do tasks very quickly and to a high standard; may be cost effective for large volumes of tasks; specialist equipment is available

Test your progress

Use the questions to test your progress.

1. What piece of **software** could be used to produce a staff handbook?

....

2. Name three pieces of **equipment** which could be used to produce a staff handbook.

....

....

3. A photocopier can produce single-sided copies. Give two more examples of how a photocopier can be used.

....

....

4. Advise the new reprographics assistant on what equipment and software could be used to complete the following:

    a) Fire regulations posters ....

    b) Property schedules (for an estate agent)..

5. How could photographs be included in the organisation's monthly newsletter?

....

....

CREDIT

6. An organisation uses a computer and a black and white printer to produce its promotional leaflets. Justify the use of two more pieces of equipment which would ensure a high quality leaflet.

....

....

7. An organisation is unsure whether to produce their sales catalogue within the organisation or to use an external agency. Make a recommendation with justification.

....

....

8. Reprographics staff are unsure how to use a new piece of equipment and what to do if it breaks down. What should be done? Justify your answer.

....

....

Answers

1. Word processing; desktop publishing (DTP)

2. Printer; photocopier; scanner; digital camera; laminator; binder

3. Copies can be made onto paper, card or OHP transparencies and in various sizes – A5, A4, A3; back-to-back copies can be made; multi-page documents can be collated/stapled; documents can be enlarged or reduced in size, or darkened/lightened; colour copies can be produced; can be linked to PC to produce colour copies directly from the computer

4. a) Software: word processing; desktop publishing (DTP): Equipment: Printer to produce one/several hard copy/ies; photocopier to allow several copies to be made: laminator to protect the posters:
b) Software: word processing; desktop publishing (DTP) could be used: Equipment: digital camera to allow photographs to be included: scanner to allow graphics to be included: printer to produce a hard copy; photocopier to produce/collate/staple several copies: laminator to protect the documents

5. Use a digital camera or a scanner

6. Colour printer to produce a colour version of the leaflets: photocopier to allow several copies to be made: digital camera to allow photographs to be included: scanner to allow graphics to be added. Justification: all of these improve the appearance of the leaflets: make the leaflets more appealing to potential customers

7. Recommendation 1: Produce the sales catalogue in-house. Justification: tasks can be completed quickly – no delay in sending work to and waiting for its return: in-house tasks can be prioritised and 'fed in': cheaper than using an external agency. Recommendation 2: Use an external agency. Justification: equipment currently available within organisation may not be capable of completing the task to a high standard: cost to organisation of purchasing new equipment is high: employees must be trained to use equipment which may be costly in time and money: equipment must be maintained: external agency is able to provide specialist equipment and staff who are trained and expert in tasks involved: specialist staff are able to complete tasks very quickly and to a high standard: it may be cost effective for large volumes of tasks

8. Staff working within the Reprographics Department must be trained in the use of new equipment for the following reasons (justification): so that they know how to use the equipment safely; to know what to do in the event of a fault; to be able to use the equipment efficiently – producing high quality output and reducing waste; to be familiar with appropriate legislation – copyright laws

Sources of information 1

An Administration Assistant will be required to know where to find information – it may be information relating to the organisation, such as holiday entitlement of staff or details of products, or it may be information to be gained from outwith the organisation, such as travel and accommodation information or current (business) news.

Sources of information can be people-based, paper-based or ICT (Information and Communications Technology)-based – also known as electronic sources of information.

People-based sources of information

People-based information is gathered through direct contact with other people, such as face-to-face meetings, telephone conversations, etc. A disadvantage with this method is that sometimes no formal record is kept of what was discussed (unless minutes were taken at meeting). Without formal documentation it is possible for conversations to be misinterpreted or even forgotten.

Paper-based sources of information

Most organisations have access to electronic sources of information, but an Administrative Assistant should be aware that there are times when paper-based sources of information will be the more appropriate method, for example, if access to the internet is not available.

Paper-based sources of information include reference books, directories, leaflets, brochures, newspapers, timetables, catalogues, files – anything that is printed. Some examples of paper-based sources and their uses are given below.

Top Tip
Recent exam questions have focused on the use of paper-based sources of information – naming the source and stating what it would be used for.

Top Tip
One disadvantage of paper-based sources of information is that the information can go out of date quickly.

Source of Information	Information contained	Uses
• Whitaker's Almanack; Pears Cyclopaedia	• Reference books covering British and world affairs for a particular year	• Information on world events, history, people
• Who's Who	• Short biographies of famous people	
• (Roget's) Thesaurus	• Synonyms and antonyms (words which mean the same or the opposite)	• Preparing a report or memo
• Dictionary	• Spelling and meaning of words	
• Timetables (bus, train)	• Departure and arrival times of buses, trains etc.	• Arranging business travel

Source of Information	Information contained	Uses
• Hotel brochure or directory (for a particular hotel organisation)	• Lists hotels and their facilities	• Finding accommodation
• Road map	• Alternative routes	• Planning route
• Newspapers • Magazines (trade), catalogues	• Current affairs • Up-to-date information on new products, equipment, etc.	• Keeping abreast of current developments

ICT sources of information

Electronic or ICT sources of information are those which can be accessed using ICT equipment, such as CD-Rom, database, spreadsheet, teletext, internet and intranet.

CD-Rom

Many reference books can now be obtained in CD-Rom format, for example, telephone directories. These have many of the drawbacks of traditional reference books – they can go out of date quickly and they may be costly to replace.

Database

Internal information including staff records, training records, customer records, supplier records, etc. can all be held on databases. The information can be searched and filtered to produce customised reports.

External databases are databases created by one company and made available or sold to other organisations. An organisation might purchase such information to help identify potential customers.

Spreadsheets

Internal information including departmental budgets, sales records, price lists, etc. can be stored in spreadsheet applications. The information can be sorted and edited to produce customised reports.

Teletext

Teletext is useful for current information on travel conditions, news, weather, etc.

Quick Test

1. State one disadvantage of people-based information.
2. Give an instance of when paper-based sources of information may be more appropriate than using the internet.
3. What is one disadvantage of paper-based sources of information?
4. Give two examples of electronic sources of information.

Answers 1. Conversations can be misinterpreted or forgotten unless a record is kept **2.** When the internet is not available **3.** They can go out-of-date quickly; can be costly to replace **4.** CD-Rom; database; spreadsheet; teletext; internet; intranet

Sources of information 2

Internet

The internet has many uses for an organisation:

- advertising the organisation, its products and job vacancies
- **electronic commerce** (**e-commerce**) – customers find a product, then order and pay for it using credit/debit card
- keeping up to date with information about competitors – their products and prices
- using e-mail to contact customers and sales representatives
- researching and booking travel, accommodation, car hire, etc.

An organisation may set up its own website in order to increase sales because the website will be available to existing and potential customers 24 hours a day, 7 days a week, all over the world.

A good website will have these features:

- **up-to-date information** on products (a nominated person could be responsible for **regularly** updating website or amending the website as soon as a change occurs e.g. change in price)
- easy to navigate – **hyperlink**s should be available and a **search facility** to locate particular products/information may be useful
- e-commerce facility should be available if appropriate
- frequently asked questions (FAQ) section
- contact details of organisation/e-mail link to organisation
- easy-to-remember URL (website address).

Terms associated with the internet

- **Internet service provider** (ISP) – a company that provides access to the internet.
- **Download** – the process of copying a document or other type of file from the internet to a personal computer.
- **Search engine** – a facility that lets the user type in a key word or phrase and creates a list of relevant websites for the user to access.
- **Hyperlink** – a connection from one web page or site to another web page or site, or to a film, sound file, a picture or program. It is usually a highlighted word but can be a picture; when over a hyperlink, the cursor usually changes from an arrow to a hand.
- **Favourites** – a facility of web browsers that lets the user store the addresses of web pages which are visited frequently.

Top Tip
Practice using the internet to locate information, including using a search engine, as you may be asked to do this in your practical abilities project

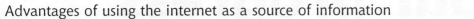

Advantages of using the internet as a source of information

- Information is usually up-to-date.
- Using a search engine and key words/phrases allows access to a wide range of information, even if the user does not know specific URLs.
- The internet is available 24 hours a day, 7 days a week – this allows it to be used at a time convenient to the user.
- Websites may give more detailed information than a brochure, for example, pictures or video clips of hotels.
- Information is available instantly, for example, availability and price quotations; bookings can be made on-line using credit/debit cards; and confirmation can be received via e-mail.

Problems associated with using the internet as a source of information

- Individuals can easily set up their own website – there is no guarantee these websites will contain accurate information.
- Websites need to be updated regularly if they are to be reliable – out-of-date timetables, prices, etc. can inconvenience the user.
- Sometimes internet connections or websites are unavailable.

Top Tip

An organisation should promote its website by including the website address on company letterheads, business cards, advertising materials, etc.

Intranet

An intranet is an **internal network** used to share information within an organisation. It can only be accessed by the organisation's employees. The intranet may be used for:

- up-to-date company information, for example, internal telephone directory
- up-to-date product information, for example, price lists
- daily or weekly bulletins and announcements
- internal e-mail
- electronic diary facilities – useful for finding suitable times for meetings
- sharing software.

Advantages of an intranet

- The same information is available to all employees – policy documents, training packages, etc.
- Information needs to be updated only once.
- Standardised documents can be stored and accessed by all employees.
- Fewer documents are photocopied for circulation, saving paper and costs.

Quick Test

1. Define the term 'hyperlink'.
2. Why might sales increase if an organisation has a website?
3. Justify the use of an intranet.

Answers 1. Connection from one web page or site to another web page or site, or to a film, sound file, a picture or program. **2.** Website is available to more potential customers; if e-commerce is available, customers can order online **3.** All employees have access to same information; information needs updating only once; standardised documents available; saves paper and costs

Test your progress

Use the questions to test your progress.

1. Name and describe two paper-based sources of information which could be used when preparing reports and memos.

....

....

2. Michael Higgins, Office Manager at Gael Printing, uses the internet to research and book travel. Recently, he has experienced problems with the internet. Advise Michael on how he could use paper-based sources of information to research and book travel.

....

....

....

3. What are the drawbacks of relying on a CD-Rom for information?

....

4. State four ways in which an organisation could make use of the internet.

....

....

....

....

....

5. Define the term 'e-commerce' (electronic commerce).

....

6. Describe two features of a good website.

....

....

7. Cleland Aquatic Centre has a website which it uses to advertise its products. Recently the following problems have arisen. Suggest how they could be avoided in future.

a) The website contains out-of-date information.

....

b) Customers have complained that they cannot buy goods online.

....

c) Many people are unaware that Cleland Aquatic Centre has a website.

....

Equipment

Data projector

A data projector allows images to be displayed from a computer monitor onto a screen, enabling information to be viewed by an audience.

Overhead projector

An overhead projector is used to show acetates (OHP transparencies) onto a large screen, again allowing information to be viewed by an audience.

Interactive whiteboard

An interactive whiteboard allows data to be displayed to a large audience and manipulated (changed) during the presentation.

Flipchart

A flipchart can be used to show information previously prepared to a smaller audience or may be used to highlight points discussed at meetings. Used frequently for training purposes.

TV and video

TV and video can be linked to a large screen to be shown to an audience. Useful for training purposes, such as demonstration of new procedures.

Scanner and digital camera

These can be used to incorporate pictures/graphics/maps to enhance a presentation.

Top Tip

When defining a term in the exam, you will not get any marks if you simply repeat part of the term, for example, saying that a data projector 'projects'. You must use different wording to show you understand the term and gain full marks.

Quick Test

1. Name two types of software applications that may be used to enhance presentations.

2. State one use of a data projector when giving a presentation.

3. Why would an interactive whiteboard be used during a presentation?

4. Give an example of when a TV or video could be used to present information.

Answers 1. Presentation/word processing/desk top publishing/spreadsheet software **2.** Allows images to be shown directly from a computer monitor to a screen **3.** User can change information during the presentation **4.** To demonstrate new procedures

Test your progress

Use the questions to test your progress.

1. Give one use of each of the following types of charts or graphs.

   a) Bar chart...

   ....

   b) Line graph..

   ....

   c) Pictogram...

   ....

2. Complete the following table.

Form	Use
Travel/Accommodation Request Form	
Itinerary	
Travel Expenses Claim Form	

3. List three examples of when members of staff may be required to give a presentation.

....

....

....

....

4. What is meant by the term 'enhancing the presentation'?

....

....

....

....

5. Explain how each of the following software applications could be used to enhance a presentation.

   a) Presentation software

   ....

   b) Word processing/Desktop publishing software

   ....

6. Explain how each of the following items of equipment could be used to enhance a presentation.

   a) Data projector..

   b) Interactive whiteboard..

   c) Flipchart...

7. Give two examples of when a report might be written.

   ....

   ....

   ....

8. How could you ensure a report is professionally produced?

   ....

   ....

   ....

CREDIT

Answers

8. It should be prepared on word processing software and incorporate graphs, tables, graphics, etc.

7. To describe the need to purchase new equipment/machinery; to give a solution to an identified problem (e.g. health and safety); to recommend a new procedure be implemented; to recommend the organisation expands into new markets

6. a) Allows images to be projected directly from a computer monitor to a screen, so information can be viewed by an audience:
   b) Allows data to be displayed to a large audience and manipulated during the presentation:
   c) Can be used to show already prepared information to a smaller audience or may be used to highlight points discussed at meetings

5. a) Each slide contains relevant information, including graphics and can be animated; sound and video clips can be incorporated; slides can be set to automatically move on to the next slide or they can be moved on with the click of a mouse:
   b) Used to prepare presentation; graphics can be used to enhance the presentation

4. Make it more interesting, look better, easier to understand and read

3. The Training Officer may deliver induction or in-service courses to staff; the Sales Manager may give a presentation on the latest sales figures to the Managing Director; the Managing Director may give a presentation to shareholders on how well the company is performing

2. Travel/Accommodation Request form: completed by an employee going on business trip, so that the administrator organising the trip receives accurate and relevant information. Itinerary: contains details of a business trip (e.g. transport and accommodation information, details of meetings, contact details). Travel Expenses Claim form: completed by an employee to ensure that they are reimbursed for any expenses they incurred while on company business

1. a) To show comparisons over short periods of time or between different products or branches; to compare actual and target sales figures:
   b) To compare actual and projected figures; to identify trends, e.g. sales figures over a period of time:
   c) When only a quick, general impression is needed

Arrangements 1

Reasons for business travel

People within an organisation may need to travel to attend meetings and conferences, to receive training, or to visit customers, suppliers or other branches of the organisation.

A **Travel Administrator** is usually responsible for making travel arrangements. Some organisations may use a **Travel Agent** as they have more experience and expertise in this area.

Making travel arrangements

In order to make the most appropriate travel arrangements, the Travel Administrator must gather the following information:

- name(s) of employee(s) travelling
- start and finish dates of the trip
- destination
- purpose of the trip
- any specific arrangements to be made during the trip – conference details, places to visit
- preferred method of travel

- whether accommodation is needed
- special requirements – disabled facilities, vegetarian meal options
- budget
- company policy (such as only senior management being allowed to travel first class).

Employees may be asked to complete a **Travel/Accommodation Request Form** to help the Travel Administrator gather all the necessary information.

Top Tip
You may be asked to prepare or complete a Travel/Accommodation Request Form in the Practical Abilities project or to complete one which has been partially completed in the KU/PS paper (at Foundation level).

Choosing a method of transport

There are four main methods of transport:
- road – private or company car, hire car, taxi or bus
- rail – local, national or international (e.g. Eurostar) train
- sea – ferry, seacat or hovercraft
- air – domestic or international airlines.

The method of transport chosen will depend on:
- destination/distance
- reason for the trip
- who is travelling and their preferred method of travel
- amount of time available
- budget
- company policy.

Finding travel information

The Travel Administrator can use a number of sources of information to help them make necessary arrangements.

Source of information	Justification for using this source
Timetables – airline, bus, train	• To calculate length of time of journey • To find out departure/arrival times
Travel guides	• To provide employee with local information – places to visit, eat, currency, time differences
Maps (local street maps and national map)	• To allow a route to be planned • To allow the employee to find their way from station to hotel
CD-Roms (containing route planners, hotel guides)	• To allow a route to be planned • To provide information on facilities available within different hotels
Hotel directories (providing details on star ratings, facilities and costs)	• To allow a comparison to be made between all the hotels available in the area
Hotel guides (to provide information on a chain of hotels)	• To provide information on facilities available within different hotels • To provide locations of hotels within a chain
Travel agents	• To provide expertise and advice in making travel arrangements • To book travel/accommodation, possibly at a discounted rate
Internet	• To allow access to online information on timetables, hotel guides, route planners • To compare prices, suitability, availability of different options • To make online bookings

Top Tip

At Credit level you will always be asked to justify how travel arrangements should be made.

Quick Test

1. Give one reason why employees need to travel.

2. What is the purpose of a Travel/Accommodation Request Form?

3. Can an employee travel using any method of transport? Give reasons for your answer.

4. Travel information can be found using paper-based sources. Name two other sources of information used in making travel arrangements.

5. Justify the use of the internet as a source of information for making travel arrangements.

Answers 1. To attend meetings or conferences; receive training; visit customers, suppliers or other branches. 2. To help Travel Administrator gather all the necessary information to make suitable travel arrangements. 3. No; the method of transport will depend on: destination; distance; reason for the trip; who is travelling and the preferred method of travel; amount of time available; budget; company policy. 4. Travel agents; electronic sources such as CD-Rom or internet. 5. To allow access to online information on timetables, hotel guides, route planners; to compare different options (prices, suitability, availability); to make online bookings for travel or accommodation.

Arrangements 2

Making arrangements

An employee must complete a Travel/Accommodation Request Form to help the Travel Administrator gather all the necessary information for making suitable travel arrangements. The Travel Administrator will then use a variety of sources of information to research the most suitable travel and accommodation for the trip.

Once the method of travel has been chosen, the Travel Administrator will complete a **Travel booking Form** and send it to the travel provider, for example, the Travel Agent.

Once the hotel and type of accommodation have been chosen, the Travel Administrator will complete an **Accommodation Order Form** and send it to the chosen hotel or Travel Agent.

If bookings are made by telephone or using the internet, then the Travel Administrator must confirm the bookings in writing. This can be done by e-mail or by sending a fax (this is the quickest way to confirm a booking). If the booking is in advance then a letter of confirmation could be sent by post.

Once all the travel and accommodation arrangements have been made the Travel Administrator will prepare an **Itinerary**. This provides important information on travel, accommodation and other arrangements (including contact details). It is organised in **chronological order** (date and time).

A good Itinerary should:

- allow time between appointments for travel or refreshment breaks
- allow time after travelling for relaxation
- take into account time differences
- always be shown in 24 hour clock and at local times
- provide information on check-in times and flight numbers
- provide contact details and addresses of people to meet and hotels.

Top Tip

In the Practical Abilities project you may be asked to use the internet to search for suitable travel arrangements and then prepare an Itinerary.

What the employee needs for business travel

Any employee who is going on a business trip should have:

- details and confirmation of all the travel/accommodation arrangements
- travel tickets (possibly an e-ticket – printed from the internet)
- all necessary paperwork – documents required for meetings, notes for presentations, etc.

Special arrangements

Sometimes special arrangements are made for employees, particularly if they are travelling abroad. It is the responsibility of the Travel Administrator to find out what is required and ensure that the employee has the relevant documentation and immunisations.

Possible requirement	Justification
Passport	Anyone travelling outside the UK requires a valid passport.
Visa	Certain countries insist on a visa for entry, for example, some countries outside Europe.
Immunisation form	This certifies that the person has the relevant immunisations (a requirement to visit certain countries outside Europe).
EHIC (European Health Insurance Card)	This allows a person to get reduced cost/free medical treatment if needed while travelling in Europe.
UK/International driving licence	To allow a person to drive/hire a car (abroad).
Travel insurance	This is required to cover the cost of unforeseen circumstances – personal, health and travel.
Company or personal credit/debit cards	To pay for items while travelling (see page 74).
Phone cards	To allow the employee to contact home/organisation.
Itinerary	This is usually prepared by the Travel Administrator (it is not an official document). It provides important information on travel, accommodation and arrangements.

Top Tip
EHIC was previously called E111 Form – you must now use EHIC when answering any exam questions.

Quick Test

1. A hotel room has been booked for tonight and must be confirmed.
   a) How can this be done?
   b) Justify your answer.

2. What document should be given to an employee to provide them with all the relevant information for their trip?

3. What is an e-ticket?

4. Explain the purpose of an EHIC.

5. What documentation is required by an employee visiting Africa?

Answers 1. a) Confirmation may be made by fax or e-mail **b)** The booking is for tonight so confirmation must be made and received immediately; a letter by post would not get there in time **2.** Itinerary **3.** A travel ticket printed from the internet following an online booking **4.** Insurance which allows a person to get reduced cost or free medical treatment while travelling in Europe **5.** Passport; visa and immunisation form (as required by specific countries); travel insurance; travel tickets; international driving licence (if planning to drive or hire car)

Paying for travel

Methods of payment

Account

When an organisation uses a Travel Agent, the Travel Agent usually sends the organisation an **account** or invoice for all travel/accommodation costs on a regular basis. The organisation's Travel Administrator or Finance Department would verify (check) the invoice and organise payment.

Alternatively, if the organisation regularly uses a particular hotel chain, they may have an account with them. This means that when employees stay at that hotel, they do not pay for it at the time; instead an invoice is sent directly to the organisation for payment.

Business credit card and business debit card

Business credit cards allow employees to purchase goods and services while travelling on company business which the organisation will pay for at a later date. The business credit card bill is sent to the organisation and the Finance Department will pay it once it is verified.

Business debit cards allow employees to pay for goods and services while travelling on company business, but the amount is deducted immediately from the organisation's bank account. The bank sends a Statement of Account to the Finance Department on a regular basis, and all purchases and expenditure would be checked.

There are a number of advantages of using business credit/debit cards:

- Employees do not need to carry large sums of cash.
- The employee is not out of pocket for business expenses.
- Business credit card bills and Statements of Accounts are usually itemised – the organisation can use these to check against receipts to verify expenditure.
- The organisation can control spending by placing a limit on business credit/debit card expenditure.

Business credit/debit cards are useful for paying for common business travel expenses (flights, hotel accommodation, meals, etc.).

Top Tip
Questions in exams often ask for benefits of cards to the business or the employee. Ensure your answer is specific to the question.

Other methods of payment

Unlike a credit card, the expenses charged to a **charge card** (for example, American Express) must be paid in full at the end of each month. They have many of the benefits of using business credit/debit cards.

Business cheques can be used for paying travel expenses. Money is deducted from the organisation's bank account a few days after the cheque has been deposited in the payee's bank account. Business cheques usually require the signatures of a couple of senior employees in the organisation.

An employee may use their own **cash** or currency to pay for small items of expenditure while on a business trip, such as taxi fares. They should keep any relevant receipts and complete a **Travel Expenses Claim form** on their return in order to have their travel expenses reimbursed.

> **Traveller's cheques** can be obtained in advance of travelling to a foreign country. In certain countries (such as the USA) traveller's cheques can be used as an alternative to local currency. In other countries they must be exchanged for local currency at a local exchange bureau.

Travel Expenses Claim form

If an employee wishes to claim back any expenses incurred on their business travel they should complete a Travel Expenses Claim form. They need to check that any expenses claimed are in line with company policy and that all relevant receipts are attached to the claim form.

The Finance Department would be responsible for checking and verifying expenditure (that is, checking that the employee has not claimed for anything outwith their allowance or budget). They also check receipts and calculations before reimbursing the employee.

There are a number of benefits of using Travel Expenses Claim forms

- employees are aware of what can be claimed for and what must be submitted in order to claim expenses
- it is easier for Finance staff to check and verify expenditure if a standard form is used by all employees
- it is easier for an organisation to monitor and analyse expenditure.

Top Tip
Travel Expenses Claim forms can be produced using spreadsheet software; using formulae allows automatic calculations, reducing the chance of errors.

Quick Test

1. Give one example of when a business credit card might be used.

2. When might it be appropriate to use cash to pay for business expenses?

3. What form should an employee complete to ensure their travel expenses are reimbursed?

Answers 1. Paying for flights, accommodation, meals **2.** To pay for small items of expenditure, such as taxi fares **3.** Travel Expenses Claim form

Test your progress

Use the questions to test your progress.

1. Give an example of a special request which could be made by an employee on a Travel Request Form.

   ....

2. Name two travel documents which an employee should take on a business trip.

   ....

3. What special arrangements would have to be made for an employee travelling to India?

   ....

   ....

4. Name three different pieces of information which would be found in an Itinerary.

   ....

   ....

5. What documentation would be completed by a Travel Administrator to book a hotel room?

   ....

6. Gillian Smith is the Sales Manager of Boyd Enterprises, Carluke. On 17 January 2007, Gillian attended a sales conference in Newcastle. Use the following information to complete the Travel Expenses Claim Form below.

   Distance from Carluke to Newcastle: 142 miles; petrol claim 40p/mile

Spice Restaurant
17 Jan 2007
Food £16.45
Drink £7.00
Total £23.45
Paid by Credit Card
Signed Gillian Smith

Candle's Hotel, 54 Quay Lane, Newcastle		
Ref. No.: 001232		
Date	Details	Cost
17/01/07	Double room en-suite	£145.00
Paid by credit card ****3027		
Signed: Gillian Smith		

TRAVEL EXPENSES CLAIM FORM

Employee name: _____ Dept: _____

Date of trip: _____

Purpose of trip: _____

Details of expenses (description and cost) £ p

Travel expenses

_____

Accommodation expenses

_____

Additional expenses

_____

Total expenses due: _____

Signed: *Gillian Smith*

Please ensure all receipts are attached to this form before being submitted to the Finance Department

7. Justify the use of paper-based sources of information when making travel arrangements.

....

8. Suggest and justify two documents (other than a passport) which an employee would need when travelling to France on business.

....

Answers

1. Disabled facilities; vegetarian meal options; internet access; ground floor room

2. Tickets; confirmation of accommodation reservation; passport; visa; EHIC; travel insurance; itinerary

3. Arrange visa, check if immunisations required

4. Name of person going on trip; date of trip; destination; reason for trip; flight details; accommodation details; meeting arrangements; dinner arrangements; contact details

5. Accommodation Booking form

6. Form appropriately completed with following information: Employee name: Gillian Smith; Dept: Sales; Date of trip: 17/01/07; Purpose: attend sales conference; Travel expenses: petrol (284 miles @ £0.40/mile = £113.60); Accommodation: 1 night, Candle's Hotel, Newcastle, £145.00; Additional: Dinner at Spice Restaurant, £23.45; Total: £282.05

7. Timetables: to calculate the length of time required for journey; to find out departure/arrival times; travel guides: to give employee local information; maps: to allow a route to be planned; hotel directories: to compare hotels available within a particular area

8. Travel (flight/train/ferry) tickets: so employee can travel by chosen method; EHIC: so employee can get reduced cost/free medical treatment if necessary; international driving licence: to allow employee to drive/hire a car in France; travel insurance: to cover the cost of unforeseen circumstances when in France

Knowledge and Understanding /Problem Solving

- **Knowledge and Understanding** is the ability to recall, describe and explain facts related to the Standard Grade Administration course.
- **Problem Solving** is the ability to use information gained throughout the course to provide solutions to specific problems.

Hints for the KU/PS exam

- Take time to read the questions fully and consider your answer carefully before committing your answer to paper.
- Although marks are not deducted for poor spelling or untidy work, it can make it difficult for a marker to actually read and therefore allocate marks to correct points – try to be as neat and tidy as possible.
- One-word answers are unlikely to gain marks. Similarly, the terms 'quick and easy' and 'neater' are unlikely to gain marks unless they have been backed up with relevant information.
- When answering problem solving questions it is usually best to write your answer as a complete sentence.
- Ensure that your suggestion can actually **solve** the problem. **Listing features is not acceptable** as this does not actually solve the problem, for example:

  Problem: Computer operators are complaining of backache.

  Solution: Adjustable chairs.   ✗ Unacceptable solution

  Solution: Provide/purchase adjustable chairs.   ✓ Acceptable solution

Top Tip
When answering problem solving questions the following verbs are often useful: install, purchase, provide, introduce, use.

- **Pay particular attention to highlighted words in questions – these give you extra guidance on what is required in your answer, for example, 'State one advantage of homeworking.'**
- **Your answer must relate to the question set, so read the question carefully. In particular, check whether it refers to the employee or employer. Candidates often misread these terms and do not answer the actual question asked – and so gain no marks.**
- **If a question asks for tasks undertaken by an employee in a specific department, you must answer accordingly – you will not gain marks if your answers simply describes a 'general' task undertaken by a manager, administration assistant, etc. You must relate your answer to the department and name a task which would be undertaken by an employee at that level in that department.**

Top Tip
Exam questions often ask for definitions of terms. Make sure you can define particular terms well, for example, chain of command, e-commerce.

Foundation level

For problem solving questions you may be given the start of the answer, for example:

> *Problem:* Harry Handsome often has headaches while working on the computer.
>
> Harry Handsome should ....

Always read the start of the sentence. When you complete your answer, make sure **the whole sentence makes sense**.

Credit level

At Credit level, you must **justify** your choices or recommendations in order to gain the highest possible marks. Justifying your answer means **explaining why** you feel the suggestion you have provided is the best option. At this level problem solving questions tend to be worth two marks each. One mark is given to a suggestion for solving the problem and one mark is given to the justification.

Justifying answers

Problem	Solution	Justification
A suspicious parcel has been left in reception.	Inform security	They are experts who have been trained to deal with this type of situation.
All employees can access confidential information which they do not require.	Password-protect confidential files	Only authorised personnel should gain access to this information as it is confidential.
Staff wages are calculated manually and errors have been made.	Use a spreadsheet package	Correctly entered formulae automatically and accurately calculate wages.
Parker plc wish to produce high quality sales brochures but are unsure whether to do this in-house or use an external agency.	Use an external agency	They will use latest technology and equipment and employ expert staff which will ensure brochures are high quality.
The Finance Department within RockRig plc is unsure which method of filing to use.	Use numerical method of filing	Invoices can be given reference numbers and filed according to this number. Numerical filing systems are easy to expand.
Staff at Strachan plc work in an open plan office environment. Staff work rate has fallen recently.	Introduce carrels, hot rooms	These allow staff to concentrate (if office is noisy) in order to complete tasks.

Top Tip
When justifying your answer ensure you do not repeat the question as the reason for the justification.

Foundation level

1.

Marion Smith
Managing Director

James Boyd	Alistair Black	Mhairi Farrell	Harriet Brown
Sales Manager	*Purchasing Manager*	*Finance Manager*	*Human Resources Manager*
Paul Dolan	Helen Miller	Vicky Jones	Elaine Scott
Sales Assistant	*Purchasing Assistant*	*Finance Assistant*	*Human Resources Assistant*

a) State the **job title** of the employee who is directly responsible for the Finance Assistant.

.... (KU 1)

b) Paul Dolan needs urgent help with a sales problem. James Boyd is in a meeting and cannot be contacted.

Paul Dolan should .... (PS 1)

c) How many members of staff is Marion Smith, Managing Director, directly responsible for?

.... (KU 1)

d) Name one other piece of information which could have been included in this organisation chart.

.... (KU 1)

e) State one task that would be carried out by Harriet Brown, Human Resources Manager, on a regular basis.

.... (KU 1)

2. Below is a list of tasks.

  A Send catalogues to customers

  B Complete order forms to buy goods required by the organisation

  C Check Travel Expenses Claim forms

  D Update employee records

Match **each** of the tasks above with the departments in the table. The first one has been done for you.

	Department	Letter of task
(i)	Personnel/Human Resources	D
(ii)	Purchases	
(iii)	Finance	
(iv)	Sales	

(KU 3)

3. Indicate which of the following statements are TRUE or FALSE by placing a tick (✓) in the appropriate box.

	Statement	TRUE	FALSE
A	Carrels can be used in an open-plan office layout to allow confidential meetings to take place		✓
B	Hot desks must be booked in advance		
C	Noise can be a problem in an open-plan office		

(KU 3)

4. a) Identify 2 common problems associated with working with ICT equipment.

Problem 1 ....

Problem 2 .... (KU 2)

b) For each of the problems identified above, suggest a solution for preventing them in future.

Solution 1 ....

Solution 2 .... (PS 2)

5. a) State two duties of a receptionist.

....

....

....

.... (KU 2)

b) Why is it important that the receptionist is well groomed and efficient?

....

.... (KU 1)

c) Name one item of equipment used by a receptionist on a regular basis.

.... (KU 1)

6. The following items of mail have to be sent today, but the Mail Room Assistant is unsure how to send them. Delete the incorrect answer by scoring it out. The first one has been done for you.

	Mail to be sent	Send by
(i)	Letter to customer about next week's sale	First class post/~~Fax~~
(ii)	Confidential sales figures	E-mail/second class post
(iii)	Urgent confirmation of an order	First class post/Fax
(iv)	Sales catalogues	Courier/E-mail

(PS 3)

7. a) State the method of filing used opposite.

....

.... (KU 1)

b) The Filing Department has said that this method of filing is not suitable as it can be difficult to locate files easily. How could this problem be overcome?

....

.... (PS 1)

8. Ultimate Parties store their supplier records on database.

SUPPLIER DATABASE : Table

COMPANY NAME	ADDRESS LINE 1	TOWN	GOODS SUPPLIED
Disco Divas	3 Newton Lane	PAISLEY	Entertainment
Treats Are Us	408 Grate Lane	GLASGOW	Cakes, Favours
Smashing Parties	32 Ardrossan Road	SALTCOATS	Bouncy Castles
Birthday Bashes	5 South Avenue	GREENOCK	Entertainment
Fun Parties	88 Glen Lane	WISHAW	Bouncy Castles
Party Party Party!	5 Edmont Crescent	AIRDRIE	Entertainment

a) How many fields are shown on the above database?

.... (KU 1)

b) Ultimate Parties cannot contact their suppliers urgently. Suggest how this database could be changed to allow Ultimate Parties to overcome this problem.

Ultimate Parties could .... (PS 1)

c) How could Ultimate Parties find out all suppliers of entertainment using the database?

Ultimate Parties could .... (PS 1)

9. The Sales Department of Amy Books plc have recently installed a new computer system. The following problems have been identified. For each problem suggest a solution.

Problem 1: Staff have difficulty finding files they have been working on.

Solution 1: Amy Books plc should .... (PS 1)

Problem 2: All staff can access confidential information.

Solution 2: Amy Books plc should .... (PS 1)

10. The following diagram was prepared by Antony, Managing Director of Antony's Soccer School.

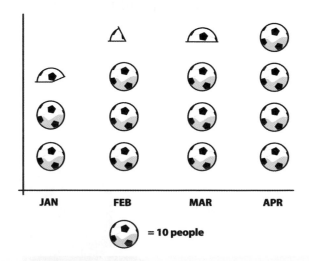

a) Name this type of diagram.

.... (KU 1)

b) Name one other type of diagram that Antony could use to show this information.

.... (KU 1)

11. Below is a list of sources of information.

Timetable

Dictionary

Hotel guide

Trade magazine

Match **each** source of information with their use in the table opposite. The first one has been done for you.

(KU 3)

	Use	Source of information
(i)	When buying new equipment – to find out the latest models	Trade magazine
(ii)	To find out departure and arrival times of buses and trains	
(iii)	To prepare a report – ensures correct spelling is used	
(iv)	When organising a business trip to find accommodation with suitable facilities	

12. Frank Law, Managing Director with Comp Supplies Ltd, will be attending a meeting in Aberdeen. While in Aberdeen he wishes to stay in a 5 star hotel. The hotel must be within 1 mile of Aberdeen train station. He has also requested a ground floor room with disabled access.

The following hotels are available.

Hotel name	Star(s)	Location
Aberdeen Metro	*****	Central – 1 mile from train station
Silver Firs Hotel	****	Central – 1 mile from train station
Isla Hotel	*****	Central – 2 miles from train station

Complete the memo to Frank.

MEMORANDUM

To: Frank Law

From:

Date:

Subject:

I have reserved a room for you at the .... hotel in Aberdeen.

I have requested ....

....

as you wished.

(PS 4)

General level

1. Hamilton plc would like to provide leaflets and colour brochures containing information on its products available for sale. Describe **2** items of equipment which Hamilton plc could use to produce high quality leaflets and brochures.

....

.... (KU 2)

2. Michelle Kelly, a newly appointed Administrative Assistant with Lawrence Builders, is experiencing difficulty producing the following items.

   a) Fire regulations for display on the wall

   b) Visitor's passes.

   How could Michelle overcome these problems? Give a **different** solution for each problem.

   a) ....

   b) .... (PS 2)

3. The internet connection at Macintosh Publishing is unavailable. The travel administrator is unable to find suitable travel information.

   How could this problem be overcome using **2 different** paper-based sources of information?

   ....

   .... (PS 2)

4. One way of displaying statistical information is to use a bar chart.

   Give **another** example of how statistical information can be displayed effectively.

   .... (KU 1)

5. James McPherson is a Sales Manager at RSCL plc. He is responsible for presenting monthly sales information to staff. However, staff have complained that his presentations are boring.

   Suggest and describe 2 pieces of equipment/software that James could use in order to improve his presentations in the future.

   ....

   ....

   ....

   .... (PS 4)

6. a) What is the name of the document an employee would take on a business trip detailing all travel and accommodation arrangements?

....

.... (KU 1)

b) Give one example of a special request which may be found on a Travel/Accommodation Order Form.

.... (KU 1)

7. Murtaza Zaheer incurred expenses on his recent business trip to Paris.

a) For each expense, suggest **one** method of payment which Murtaza could use. Use a different method for each.

(i) Paying for taxi from airport ....

(ii) Paying for dinner .... (KU 2)

b) On his return, Murtaza is unsure how to claim back the money he has spent. How does he do this?

.... (PS 1)

8. Employee records of Glen plc are stored on an electronic database. An extract from the database is shown below.

EMPLOYEE RECORDS : Table			
EMPLOYEE NAME	DEPARTMENT	SALARY	DATE STARTED
Gina Mullin	Human Resources	£15,000.00	25/10/2005
Harry Hamlin	Sales	£40,000.00	03/01/1995
Petal Jason	Purchasing	£13,000.00	09/09/2006
Martin Peacock	Finance	£50,000.00	10/01/1990
Justine Smythe	Purchasing	£25,000.00	16/09/2004
Oliver Watson	Human Resources	£30,000.00	22/06/2001

Read the database and then answer the following questions.

a) What is meant by the term 'database field'?

.... (KU 1)

b) The database cannot be sorted in order of surname. Suggest one way of overcoming this problem.

.... (PS 1)

c) The field 'SALARY' has been formatted as currency. Name another way in which fields **could** be formatted.

.... (KU 1)

d) Suggest 2 advantages of storing information in a database.

....

....

....

.... (KU 2)

9. a) Explain clearly **one advantage** of a **tall organisational structure**.

.... (KU 1)

b) Explain clearly **one disadvantage** of a **tall organisational structure**.

.... (KU 1)

10. The following problems have been identified at Higgins & Taylor plc. Suggest one way in which each of the following problems could be solved. Give a **different** solution for each.

a) Staff using computers have been complaining of backache.

.... (PS 1)

b) Staff have difficulty locating files they previously saved.

.... (PS 1)

c) Confidential conversations can be overheard in the open-plan office.

.... (PS 1)

11. Describe one task which would be carried out on a regular basis by each of the following employees.

a) Finance Manager

....

b) Administration Assistant within Human Resources Department

.... (KU 2)

12. Katy Keen works in the Mail Room of Harazi plc. She is unsure how to send the following mail. Advise Katy on the most appropriate method of sending the following.

a) A change to an urgent order.

.... (PS 1)

b) Legal documents to a client.

.... (PS 1)

c) Letters informing customers of next month's sale.

.... (PS 1)

13. Anderson plc is experiencing a number of problems in the reception area. Provide solutions to the following problems. You must give a different solution for each.

a) Visitors have been found wandering in unauthorised areas.

.... (PS 1)

b) Visitors complained that the receptionist cannot answer their queries.

.... (PS 1)

c) The receptionist is unsure which staff members are in the building when a customer telephones.

.... (PS 1)

d) At a recent fire drill visitors were unsure of the procedure to be followed.

.... (PS 1)

14. Explain what is meant by the following terms:

a) Hot desk ....

b) E-commerce .... (KU 2)

7. The following concerns have been raised regarding Health and Safety at Ross & Co:

   a) Some members of staff have complained that the photocopier is unsafe.

   b) The reception area has been recently redecorated and the fire regulations posters have not been put back up on the walls.

   c) Some members of staff do not believe that health and safety is their responsibility.

What recommendations would you make to the Manager to ensure that health and safety regulations are being met?   (PS 6)

8. Employers must ensure that the workplace is a healthy and safe environment. Explain how this may be achieved.   (KU 3)

9. Justify the role of the receptionist in ensuring security within an organisation.   (KU 4)

10. A receptionist may have to deal with various security problems:

   a) a suspicious parcel being left at reception;

   b) staff arriving without ID badges;

   c) an aggressive visitor.

Suggest how the receptionist could deal with each of these problems. Justify your answers. Give a **different** answer to each problem   (PS 6)

11. Record keeping is an important part of the receptionist's duties. Suggest 2 methods of manual record keeping and justify their importance.   (KU 4)

12. An electronic diary is not only important for arranging appointments. Describe 2 other benefits of an electronic diary.   (KU 2)

13. Chloe Hume works in Head Office of Greig & Son Ltd in Glasgow. The following items of mail must be sent:

    a) A box of staff handbooks guaranteed to arrive at the Edinburgh Branch tomorrow.

    b) A DTP file containing the next monthly staff bulletin required immediately by the printers in Falkirk.

    Suggest 2 different methods of sending these items of mail and justify your answers. (PS 4)

14. Suggest and justify 2 methods of sending mail externally. You should use examples to support your answer. (KU 4)

15. Recommend an appropriate filing system for use within a busy dental practice. Justify your recommendation. (KU 3)

16. Describe the impact of the Data Protection Act on the electronic storage of data. (KU 2)

17. Storing information electronically requires the use of an effective file management system. Explain what is meant by this statement and use examples to support your answer. (KU 3)

18. a) Justify the use of 2 pieces of equipment/software which could be used by an organisation to prepare glossy sales catalogues for distribution to several hundred customers. (KU 4)

    b) Should the sales catalogues be produced in-house or using an external agency? Make a recommendation and justify your answer. (You should not mention anything already mentioned in (a).) (PS 3)

19. Explain the benefits of using the following by an organisation:

    a) Intranet

    b) Integrated software package. (KU 4)

20. Sources of information can be electronic or paper-based. Explain the benefits of using an electronic source when organising only accommodation for a business trip. (KU 3)

21. Suggest, giving reasons for your suggestions, 2 ways in which statistical information can be prepared for a presentation to staff. (KU 4)

22. A manager has received complaints about the monthly sales presentation, delivered orally, being boring and difficult to understand. Recommend 2 ways the manager could improve his presentation. Justify your answer. (PS 4)

23. Suggest and justify 2 documents which would be required by an employee while travelling within the UK. (KU 4)

24. Explain the benefits, to employees, of being issued with a company credit card. (KU 2)

25. A travel administrator is unsure of what to do when organising a business trip abroad. What advice should be given to the travel administrator? Justify your answer. (PS 6)

26. a) Explain how an organisation may use a search engine. You should use examples to support your answer. (KU 2)

   b) Explain why an organisation would make use of hyperlinks. (KU 2)

Answers to exam-style questions

Foundation level

1. a) Finance Manager
    b) Paul Dolan should go to Marion Smith/Managing Director for advice
    c) 4
    d) Telephone extension number; floor number; room number; photograph
    e) Oversees the running of the Human Resources Department; delegates tasks to staff in the Human Resources Department; interviews job applicants

2. (i) D; (ii) B; (iii) C; (iv) A

3. False; True; True

4. a) Headache; backache; RSI; eyestrain
    b) Provide antiglare screens/blinds for the windows; provide adjustable chairs; allow staff to take regular breaks; provide wrist rests/foot rests; provide regular eye tests for employees

5. a) Greeting visitors; answering telephone; updating appointments book; maintaining reception register/visitors' book; directing visitors; signing for mail
    b) To create a good impression of the organisation/first impressions are important
    c) Telephone; computer (electronic diary); intercom

6. (i) First class post/Fax; (ii) E-mail/second class post; (iii) First class post/Fax; (iv) Courier/E-mail

7. a) Numerical
    b) Change to an alphabetical filing system/use an electronic filing system

8. a) 4 fields
    b) Ultimate Parties could include e-mail addresses and/or fax/phone numbers in the database
    c) Ultimate Parties could search/filter/query the database records

9. Solution 1: Amy Books should ensure an appropriate file management system is in place; train employees in the use of file management
    Solution 2: Amy Books should provide all employees with a password

10. a) Pictogram
    b) Bar chart/pie chart/line graph

11. (i) Trade magazine; (ii) Timetable; (iii) Dictionary; (iv) Hotel guide

12. Memo correctly filled in: From: <student's name>; Date: <appropriate date>; Subject: Hotel booking; Aberdeen Metro; a ground floor room with disabled access

General level

1. (Colour) Photocopier – to produce multiple copies of leaflets/brochures; (Colour) Printer – to make original copy of leaflets/brochures; Scanner – to insert pictures of products/location map into leaflets/brochures; Digital camera – to take pictures which could be inserted into leaflets/brochures

2. a) Use Word processing/DTP software – to produce notices as graphics could be inserted/different font types and styles could be used, page borders etc.
        Also accept: colour printer – to make original (colour) copy of notice; use photocopier – to make additional copies to be placed around the organisation.
    b) Use laminator – to protect the visitor's badges from wear and tear, dirt etc.; use photocopier – to make copies of visitor badges

3. Use timetables (bus, train etc) – to find out departure and arrival times of buses, trains etc.; use hotel brochures/directories – these list all hotels in that particular chain and their facilities.; use road map – to plan various alternative routes; use travel guide – to provide further information for traveller on local information, such as currency

4. Line Graph; Pictogram, Pie Chart

5. Use PowerPoint presentation – to enhance the presentation, because PowerPoint allows the user to include animation, video clips, graphics, etc. which would make a presentation look professional and appealing.

Use data projector – to enlarge any materials prepared on computer onto a large screen, allowing all members of the audience to see the presentation clearly.
Also accept: word processing/DTP software, overhead projector, interactive whiteboard/smartboard etc. with an explanation of how they would enhance the presentation

6. a) An Itinerary
    b) If traveller requires disabled facilities, special dietary options, ground floor room, internet access, etc.

7. a) (i) Local currency; (ii) (Business) Credit/Debit Card
    b) Complete a Travel Expenses Claim form

8. a) Database fields are the searchable items in a database, they are the headings/names for each individual item of information
    b) Have 2 separate fields for names, that is, First name and Surname fields
    c) Text; Date/time; Number; Scientific
    d) Records can be found quickly using the **search** facility; Complex searches can be carried out by **searching on two fields**; Records can be arranged into required order quickly using the **sort** facility; Specific information (reports) can be gathered using the **query** facility; The **mailmerge** facility can be used to personalise letters

9. a) As they have a narrower span of control, it may be easier for managers to supervise staff; there are many opportunities for promotion; may lead to motivated employees who understand their very specific roles and responsibilities
    b) Employees may not feel involved in decisions made at top management levels; employees may not get the opportunity to show initiative; many highly paid management positions mean that it may be costly to run the business

10. a) Provide adjustable chairs for employees; ensure all employees are given regular breaks
    b) Ensure an appropriate file management system is in place; Send operators on a training course on file management
    c) Have a hot room which can be booked in advance where confidential conversations can take place

11. a) Reports to the Board of Directors on issues relating to the Finance Department; is responsible for overseeing/monitoring/motivating the employees within the Finance Department; prepares budgets and forecasts; controls spending of departments; prepares final accounts
    b) Word processes letters to successful/unsuccessful applicants; files application forms; updates and maintains employee records (on database)

12. a) Send this urgent order by fax
    b) Send legal documents to a client by Recorded Signed for postal service; Also accept: Special Delivery
    c) Send letters to customers informing them of next month's sale by second class post

13. a) Keypad locks/swipecards/locks should be put on doors which only authorised personnel have the combination/keys to; Also accept: notices should be placed around the organisation informing visitors to stay out of unauthorised areas
    b) Ensure receptionist can access all relevant information either in hard copy in a folder on desk or electronically on the intranet; Also accept: train receptionist in organisation's procedures, etc.
    c) The organisation should use a staff in/out book
    d) Place notices on evacuation procedures in reception area; Train reception staff on how to assist visitors in the event of an emergency

14. a) This is a spare desk/workstation which may be booked in advance for use by any employee;each hot desk will be equipped with a standard layout and equipment – computer and telephone
    b) Buying and selling goods online

15. a) Install an e-commerce facility/on-line order form on the website
    b) Have a nominated person whose job it is to update website whenever information has changed; ensure website is updated on a regular basis
    c) Have hyperlinks on website; have a search facility on the website

Credit level

1. **a)** Due to growth (increases or changes products/services), Decrease in size (fall in demand for products), Delayering (removing levels of management to save money), Outsourcing (using external companies to carry out specific tasks, e.g. IT support)

   b) Staff morale may fall due to fear of loss of jobs; Staff may be worried about having to learn new skills; Absenteeism may increase over fears; Increased costs due to training needs, purchase of new equipment; Decreased costs if reducing size of organisation, less staff; Improved communication if delayering, more efficient; Communication more difficult if more levels added, slowing decision making; Managers having a change of span of control

   c) Organisation chart after restructuring can show: change in size of organisation; change in chain of command; new levels of responsibility/lateral relationships; employee's new position within organisation

2. **a)** Oversees the running of the Finance Department; Reports to Board of Directors on issues within the Finance Department; Delegates tasks to the staff within the Finance Department; Carries out appraisals of staff in the Finance Department; Prepares budgets/forecasts/final accounts

   b) Completes/sends order forms; word processes letters of enquiry; files information from suppliers – catalogues, price lists; updates supplier database

3. **a)** Job description provides the applicant with information about the job – job title, salary, working conditions, etc.; this allows the applicant to decide whether or not the job suits them (does it allow flexible working, for example), and so ensures that applicants know what is expected of them before applying for the job. Only relevant people will apply, saving the organisation time and money in shortlisting applicants; the organisation interviews/appoints staff who know exactly what is required of them beforehand

   b) Person specification provides applicant with information about what qualifications, experience, skills and experience, etc. is required; applicant would use it to check that they include all the relevant qualifications, etc. in their application. An organisation would use it as a checklist to check that the applicant has the correct qualifications, etc.

4.

	Solution	Justification
a)	Change to an open plan/flexible office layout	Equipment can be shared which will save money
	Lease equipment instead of purchasing	Allows most up-to-date equipment to be used, upgrading, maintenance included
	Centralise office equipment	Equipment can be shared which will save money
b)	Set targets (bonus could be paid)	Motivates staff
	Employ a supervisor	Can monitor staff work, report back to manager
	Change to open plan/flexible office layout (provided this solution is not already given in a) above)	Allows teamworking, easier supervision
	Introduce a staff training scheme	Will improve skills and efficiency of staff making them more motivated
c)	Introduce hot desks/touchdown areas	Staff can book a desk to use when required, so fewer desks are needed, saving space and money; staff can access a touchdown area whenever necessary when visiting the office

5.

Problems	Solutions
Backache from sitting at computer for long periods of time	Ensure staff use adjustable chairs/take regular breaks
Eyestrain	Ensure that staff take regular breaks/have regular eye tests
Headaches	Ensure that staff use antiglare screens/blinds are fitted at windows/lighting is adequate/regular breaks are taken
RSI	Ensure that staff take regular breaks/use wrist rests/adjustable chairs

6. Fax – work can be prepared at home and then sent in to the office.; Can also be used to receive copies of paperwork from the office
   Mobile phone – to allow employee to keep in contact with the office (by text or voice)
   E-mail – to allow work to be prepared and then file attachments can be sent in to the office; Can also be used to receive copies of files from the office

7.

	Recommendation	Justification
a)	Equipment should be regularly checked and maintained by specialist staff/technician	Specialist staff are trained and this will prevent injury to others
	Staff should be trained in the safe use of equipment	To prevent injury
b)	Fire regulations must be on display	To allow all staff and visitors to read so they know what to do in the event of a fire
	Staff must be trained in what to do in the event of a fire	To prevent panic and to allow staff to assist with visitors in the event of evacuation
c)	Staff must be trained/kept up-to-date with training in the Health and Safety policies of the organisation	It is the responsibility of employees to look out for the health and safety of themselves and others within the organisation
	Staff must be kept informed of health and safety policies – available on the organisational intranet	To make employees aware of their responsibilities
	Remind staff of duties as per Health and Safety at Work Act 1974/Display notices of HASAWA	This Act specifically sets out responsibilities of employees in organisations

8. Provide a safe entrance/exit from work; Ensure all employees receive relevant/up-to-date training; Ensure that all equipment is safe and regularly checked/maintained; Provide protective clothing if required; Ensure that workstations meet minimum requirements; Provide cable management system

9. The receptionist is the first point of contact within an organisation. He/she may be responsible for: answering the intercom and admitting visitors to the organisation; issuing visitors' badges; ensuring that all visitors sign the reception register, operating the CCTV to monitor movement outside/within the organisation. The receptionist is able to ensure that only authorised people gain access to the organisation

10.

a)

Solution	Justification
Do not touch the parcel	It could be dangerous/harmful
Contact security/police	They are trained in what to do in this type of situation
Contact the sender of the parcel	May be able to solve the problem

b)

Solution	Justification
Issue staff with temporary badge	To allow them into the organisation for that day
Report to manager	It is a breach of company policy – requires a reprimand
Have department verify the identity of the member of staff	To confirm the identity
Have photos on file/ organisation chart	To confirm the identity

c)

Solution	Justification
Try and calm visitor	Visitor could pose a threat to staff/visitors
Contact security/manager	They are trained in what to do in this type of situation

11. Reception register/Visitor's book – used to record all visitors to the organisation; It can be used in the event of an emergency as a record of who is in the building
Staff in/out book – used to record staff entering/exiting the organisation; It can be used to identify if a member is staff is in when an enquiry is made, or in the event of an emergency
Appointments diary/book – used to record the dates/times of all appointments with staff; It will be checked when a visitor arrives and should prevent more than one visitor arriving to be seen at the same time by the same person

12. Can avoid double bookings; Can send reminders/alerts for important meetings; Regular meetings need to be keyed only once; To do list is available; Allows tasks to be prioritised; Can access several diaries for arranging meetings if on a network

13.

a)

Solution	Justification
Use Special Delivery	Guaranteed next day delivery – including parcels
Use Courier	Will ensure that parcels are delivered in time

b)

Solution	Justification
Send E-mail attachment	The only way to send a file instantly which will then allow editing

14. Fax – for sending exact copies of documents very quickly; Not suitable for confidential mail; Used for confirmation of travel arrangements, urgent order forms
E-mail – for sending information very quickly; Can include file attachments; Suitable for confidential mail; Used for references for jobs, reports for managers, memos to staff
Special Delivery – for guaranteed next day delivery which requires a signature on receipt; Used for sending original documents, e.g. legal documents
Royal Mail Postal Service – for sending non-urgent items of mail, e.g. letters to customers informing them of sale next month

15. Alphabetical filing system – records can be found very quickly as they would be stored using surnames of patients; Easy to use/understand as all patients would be stored with surnames, keeping families' records together
Numerical filing system – allows for expansion as patient numbers grow; Very easy to follow and files are less likely to be misplaced; Each patient would have a reference number
Electronic filing – allows for expansion as patient numbers grow; Takes up less space than manual filing; as records are added they can be resorted; Very easy to find records using search functions

All of the above methods are acceptable, as long as each is correctly justified

16. All organisations storing data on more than a few people must comply with the DPA; Data must be: up-to-date, obtained lawfully, not held for longer than necessary, held for a specific purpose; kept secure; Data subjects have the right to ask to see the data held on them and to ask for it to be amended if incorrect

17. File management means organising computer files so that they can be located easily; Documents should be saved using appropriate file names and should be stored in folders; Folders can be organised into different categories, e.g. all letters to job applicants could be stored in a folder called Correspondence and databases containing employees' details or applicants' details could be stored in a folder called Databases

18. a) (Colour) photocopier – to allow multiple copies of the sales catalogue to be produced which are automatically collated, stapled; (Colour) printer – to produce a high quality copy of the sales catalogue to be used as a master for copying; Digital camera – to allow photos to be taken and then inserted into the document, allowing resizing, cropping, etc.; Scanner – to allow exact copies of graphics/photos to be transferred directly to the computer, allowing resizing, cropping, etc.; Word processing package/DTP – to allow the sales catalogue to be keyed in using different colours/fonts/sizes, adding graphics, etc.

b) In-house: Printing can be specially geared towards the needs of the organisation, using their own house-style; Completion of the job can be fitted in around other work whereas sending it out may be time consuming. External agency: Wider range of equipment available in order to enhance appearance of finished item; Specialist staff are trained in use of equipment and can produce high quality catalogue quickly; No need for organisation to purchase/lease additional equipment which is costly; Allows staff to continue with other tasks.
Either of the above answers is acceptable as long as correctly justifed

19. a) The same information is available to all employees, e.g. staff handbook, policy statements, training manuals, house-styles; Equipment/software can be shared, saving money; Internal e-mail is available

b) Contains several applications (word processing, database, spreadsheet, graphics) within one program; There is a common human computer interface (layouts/menus are similar); Data can be transferred easily between applications; User can have more than one application open at the same time; Cheaper than buying several individual applications

20. The internet allows comparisons to be made between different hotels, giving clear details on facilities, costs, etc.; Information is very up-to-date; Bookings can be made on-line and confirmation made by e-mail; On-line discounts are often available, saving the organisation money; CD-Roms can go out-of-date but they do allow comparisons and give details on facilities, etc.

21. Bar chart – to show figures over a period of time, allowing comparisons to be made; Line graph – to show trends over a period of time; Pie chart – to show percentages; Pictogram – to show general information using pictures; Tables – to organise information into columns making it easier to read; Spreadsheets – to organise information into columns and creating graphs/charts

22. Use PowerPoint presentation – to enhance quality of presentation, as it includes graphics, colour, sounds; Use with multimedia projector – to allow presentation to be shown on a large screen to be seen by all employees; Use DTP/word processing software – to produce quality handouts and hold interest of employees; Use OHP – to display certain parts of presentation onto screen for all employees to see and catch their attention; Use TV/video/DVD – to demonstrate new products/ training

23. Driving licence – to allow a car to be hired; Itinerary – to provide traveller with all information required for trip; Travel tickets – to allow travel on train/bus/plane; Accommodation confirmation – to provide proof of booking

24. No need to carry cash; No need to pay for expenses then reclaim; Credit card bill is send directly to organisation, No requirement to keep receipts

25.

Advice	Justification
Request that traveller completes Travel/Accommodation Request form	To ensure that all information is available and all requirements can be met
Check budget availability	To make appropriate choices within budget
Use internet to find suitable travel/accommodation	To make comparisons, on-line discounts may be available
Use internet to book suitable travel/accommodation	To make immediate booking and send/receive confirmation by e-mail
Check what documentation is required and see if traveller has this	Certain countries require visas, EHIC required, up-to-date passport, proof of immunisation
Prepare an Itinerary	So that traveller has all relevant details for trip

26. a) A search engine could be used: to find websites where the address is not known; to find information on a particular topic; to check competitors' websites even if names of competitors or their URLs aren't known'; to find information on up-to-date employment legislation, etc.

b) Hyperlinks allow quick access to specific pages within a website/ direct links to other related websites; E-mail address can be provided as hyperlink to improve communication

Index